MATTERS OF LIFE AND FAITH

'It's calming and heartening to watch a father quietly sift his daily life for what is sacred.'

Helen Garner

'This delightful collection is a treasure chest of wisdom and experience. Paul Mitchell writes with tenderness and understated insight about the mystery of connection – whether that is with his own kids, his neighbours, strangers or the world. His words are healing and his storytelling full of wonder.'

Michael McGirr
author and Head of Mission Integration at Caritas Australia.

'Insightful and inspiring, his work underlines the things that matter most in this life through the small and everyday.'

Kerrie O'Brien
Senior Writer (Culture), *The Age*.

'There's been a renewed focus on fatherhood and masculinity in this country, and Paul's work feels particularly current and necessary, revealing how those concerns intersect with matters of faith.'

David Halliday
editor of *Eureka Street* and former editor of *The Melbourne Catholic*.

'Talk of spirituality too often hovers above the everyday, as though the aspirations of faith lift us to a "higher" plane. Not here. In this beautiful collection of stories, memories and reflections, faith and life are one. With a disarming honesty, Paul Mitchell takes us from parenting to neighbourhood fruit picking, from poetry to a hospital waiting room, from prayer to depression. Along the way he reminds us that the life we have is sacred. All of it.'

Simon Carey Holt
author and Pastor at Collins Street Baptist Church, Melbourne.

Dedicated to Jo, Hannah, Hugo and Ryland:
My words, our love and lives

'Do like it says on the mayonnaise jar: keep cool but do not freeze.'
Elizabeth Alexander

Also by Paul Mitchell

Fiction
We. Are. Family.
Dodging the Bull

Poetry
Standard Variation
Awake Despite the Hour
Minorphysics

Matters of Life and Faith

Reflections on Parenting & Everyday Spirituality

Paul Mitchell

COVENTRY PRESS

Published in Australia by
Coventry Press
33 Scoresby Road
Bayswater VIC 3153

ISBN 9780648982234

Copyright © Paul Mitchell 2021

All rights reserved. Other than for the purposes and subject to the conditions prescribed under the *Copyright Act*, no part of this publication may be reproduced, stored in a retrieval system, or transmitted in any form or by any means, electronic, mechanical, photocopying, recording or otherwise, without the prior permission of the publisher.

Scripture taken from the Holy Bible NEW INTERNATIONAL VERSION®, NIV®, Copyright © 1973, 1978, 1984, 2011 by Biblica, Inc.® Used by permission. All rights reserved worldwide.

Catalogue-in-Publication entry is available from the National Library of Australia http://catalogue.nla.gov.au

Cover design by Ian James – www.jgd.com.au
Cover image: Fleur Rendell (fleurrendell.com) from a photograph by Jo Bowers
Text design by Coventry Press
Typeset in Tex Gyre Pagella

Printed in Australia

Table of Contents

Foreword by Tony Birch		3
Introduction		6
1	Shopping for Values: A Journey with my Daughter	9
2	Dad Radio	17
3	Anzacism: A Lesson in Civil Religion	20
4	Heart Prayer	29
5	Reality Check	31
6	Father's Day Music Club	36
7	Taking the Poison out of Masculinity	39
8	Ripe for the Picking	44
9	Cuisines of the World and Crazy Thursday	49
10	Two Bobs' Worth	53
11	Play it Again. This Time with Feeling	62
12	Dad's Kitchen Rules	67
13	Memories, Like Some Corners of our Lives	71
14	UFC (Ultimate Fathering Confusion)	76
15	Punt Flick	85
16	We Have the Touch	88
17	When the Neighbourhood's Heart Broke	93

18	The Cracks in Our Stars	96
19	The Tale Food Tells	100
20	A Quartet of Hope	103
21	A Christmas Carol Confession	108
22	It's an Emergency. Take a Seat.	111
23	Competing to be Normal	117
24	Poetry with Bruce and Bunjil	121
25	The Home Monastery	124
26	Silence is Not Always Golden	127
27	Everything Under the Sun	131
28	Bill Fay: The Lowly Raised	135
29	Forever Young	139
30	The Book That Changed Me	144
31	In the Middle of the Madding Crowd	149
32	The Abbot of the Household	153
33	How to Protect the Gift	157
34	No Fear for Little Monsters	162
35	Stuck in a Moment	167
36	The Preppie	171
Acknowledgments		178

Foreword

MAKING SENSE OF THE WORLD at any time is a fraught exercise. In 2020, dealing with the COVID-19 crisis has been the challenge of a lifetime for many people. Paul Mitchell, a most thoughtful and considered writer, uses words to reflect on life. He is sometimes puzzled and frustrated by the inequities he has witnessed in recent years, aided with the ever-curious eye of an artist. He is also drawn to affection, often enacted through the most subtle and seemingly mundane gestures. Through the collection of essays gathered here, Mitchell attempts to make sense of both the most personal and universal aspects of the human condition.

Mitchell is the father of three children, two of them now independent and successful young adults. His mode of parenting, expressed through many of the essays here, is at times eccentric, occasionally tinged with struggle and always tender and loving. Reading about his interactions with his kids is reminiscent of watching a man inventing a range of parenting contraptions in a backyard shed, devices for not only surviving life but embracing it. For instance, in order to amuse and engage with his son, Mitchell is the inventor of not only 'Dad Radio' but 'Dad Airlines' – *this is your captain speaking*. He also organises both 'monster hunts' and 'shopping parties' for his children, sacrificing sanity for the happiness of his children.

To be a good father you must invest in the lives of your children beyond the role of parenting. Young kids love to play, and they love it when a parent gets down on their hands and knees and fully commits to the game. (Perhaps until they reach puberty, when an over-enthusiastic dad can become an embarrassment.) Mitchell's stories of life with his children are an exercise in juggling emotion, care, knowledge, and yes, play. He is a father who grows with his children, never losing sight of their shifting expectations of him.

Several of the essays provide moments of such tenderness that they could be missed by the casual reader. As accessible as the stories are written, I would suggest that the writing be read carefully; slow down and enjoy it. The essay, 'Shopping for Values: A Journey with my Daughter', begins as a tale about a single parent (Mitchell) taking his young daughter on a shopping expedition to Dimmey's, the dated icon of discount clothing in Victoria. The essay becomes a story about the annual pilgrimages that father and daughter make to various shopping centres, an unenviable bonding ritual.

Early in the essay, the writing touches briefly on two images of quiet emotion and beauty. The initial shopping trip is one of necessity, embarked upon after Mitchell and his wife separated. The reason he ventures into the great unknown of children's fashion is because of a need *to fill the empty cupboard in my daughter's bedroom*. A poet is at work here, filling a cupboard in not only a practical sense, but emotionally as well, building trust and care with his daughter. After the shopping trip, Mitchell's daughter *fashion-paraded every item* for her Grandma. This is both a domestic snapshot and a portrait of family, weaving love in the face of adversity.

Foreword

In another short and reflective piece, 'Poetry with Bruce and Bunjil', we come to know Paul Mitchell as both a teacher and learner. Provided the opportunity to teach poetry to Aboriginal people alongside the renowned author and ecological educator, Bruce Pascoe, Mitchell muses on the challenge of teaching, and the reward of 'breaking through' when a student shifts from their own frustrations about poetry to the revelation of the layered meanings contained in the most simple collection of words. Mitchell invests in his students and is duly rewarded. He learns that they are *nature-mystics* and that their distinct way of seeing the world offers reciprocity, with Mitchell concluding the essay with the comment *they have taught me more... have woken in me again a poetry that has nothing to do with pages, words, rhymes or Western understandings of meaning.*

I write in an attempt to make sense of a chaotic world. Sometimes I do find moments of clarity, while on other occasions I wonder if my words do little more than add to the disorder. I'm not sure what drives Paul Mitchell to write, but I would be surprised if his motivation is not similar. The essays in this collection certainly provide me with a sense of understanding. I imagine Mitchell working at times as a lens, focusing his attention on scenes of life and encouraging the reader to pause and reflect. As a parent of five adult children and three grandkids, the writing also causes me to think about my relationships with my loved ones and encourages me to reflect on a central proposition. Have I been a good father? I can only hope so.

Tony Birch
Miles Franklin short-listed for his novels *The White Girl* and *Blood*

Introduction

THE WRITING IN THIS BOOK is as close as I can get to bringing you into my life, all the snapped shoelaces and sunny picnics, dirty dishwater and clean laundry.

But that wasn't my purpose when I published these essays, and it isn't my purpose in collecting them here. I wrote them to try to understand what was happening in and around me. In publishing these often-domestic stories, I offer them as windows through which you may be able to see more clearly the mysteries, fears, hopes and joys in your own backyard.

I've tried to live by the famous quote attributed to St Irenaeus of Lyon, from which I've removed the gender reference: 'The glory of God is a person fully alive'. Trying to figure out what it is to be fully alive has led me to great joy, some of which is in these essays, but also sadness from which I thought I wouldn't recover. But I did – and it's made me think, whatever else resurrection is, it's also an everyday event, like breathing and, hopefully, laughing.

As well as the editors and publications where many of these essays first appeared, there are others to thank for making *Matters of Life and Faith* a reality.

Everyone at Coventry Press for taking a punt on a collection of essays that mixes the reasonably sacred with the not quite

Introduction

as sacred. Fine artist Fleur Rendell for her cover image, based on a photo by Jo Bowers. What a team you've made, and not just as school aftercare experts so long ago.

David Halliday, former editor of *The Melbourne Catholic*, for publishing many of these essays and encouraging me to collect them with others to form a book. Helen Garner for her endorsement, offering a sharp eye to individual works, encouraging me to write the numinous, and for enjoying her first Mint Julep in my company.

For others who've been kind to this book: thanks to Michael McGirr for his own inspiring books and articles, not least of which are his St Kevin's College newsletter yarns; Kerrie O'Brien for publishing, with Jane Willson, many of these works and for helping sculpt my ideas; Simon Holt, again for his own inspirational writing, but also his continual voice of encouragement for my work. For his Foreword, thanks to Tony Birch, who also deserves thanks for spurring me on, championing me and not letting his dog bite me too much.

To the many people who've appeared in these essays, thank you for letting me write about you. That goes, especially, for Hannah, Hugo and Ryland Mitchell. To, unfortunately, quote the '90s band Extreme, I love you three 'more than words'. And to Jo – thanks for your love and encouragement. Without you saying, 'You should write about that', half of these essays would still be in my head.

Paul Mitchell

1

Shopping for Values: A Journey with my Daughter

Soon after my first marriage broke up, I had to take my then seven-year-old daughter shopping for clothes. It had always been something she did with her mother, while I mowed the lawns or wrote. But no amount of scribbling or gardening was going to fill the empty cupboard in my daughter's bedroom. I had to get out and prowl the racks with her.

My post-divorce budget was camisole thin, so we went to Dimmey's in Geelong during summer school holidays. We were bunking with my Mum and Dad for a few days and before we left for the shops, Mum asked, 'Do you want me to take her and you can go to the beach?' The idea was appealing, but I was locked into the notion that anything my daughter's mum could do, I could do, if not better, at least capably.

She led me around every square metre of tables and racks festooned with coloured cotton, while the red lights spun their bargains and the announcements told us what we already knew: we were at Dimmey's, and we could pay less here than anywhere else for quality clothing. I wasn't sure about the Made in China quality, but I was rapt at the pricing: six bucks for two t-shirts and $12 for a pair of jeans. And, even better, it hardly mattered what I bought her; she was at an age when she couldn't have cared less about brands or what outlets her clothes came from. She worked on a variation of the Don Smallgoods theme: if they looked good, they were good.

By the end of our trip, my feet were aching. I groaned as she tried on the last of seven different kinds of eight-dollar, three-quarter length pants.

'Just pick one, sweetie. And then we're going.'

'Can I have a hot chocolate?'

Yes, ten hot chocolates. Anything to get out of here. When we eventually did arrive back at Grandma's, she fashion-paraded every item – and every possible combination of outfit – while we all ooohed and ahhhed at her style. And I forgot, as quickly as possible, about our shopping expedition.

◇ ◇ ◇

Maybe it's a reality of being a parent in a separated family, but I was often concerned I wasn't doing enough to make my children's lives okay. And how could I ever do enough? I'd denied them what they understood as a fundamental right: their two parents together, loving them in one house. No matter how resolved I became to the truth that, yes, I was doing the best I could and I couldn't make up for the past, there remained something inside me that chewed away, never far from the surface, telling me to make amends.

I suppose that accounted for my deep feeling of gratitude when I walked into my daughter's Grade Four classroom early in the school year following our shopping expedition and found hanging on the wall the poster she'd created to depict

Shopping for Values: A Journey with my Daughter

her three holiday highlights – one of which was shopping with Dad.

◊ ◊ ◊

From her birth, I'd vowed that when she grew up, my daughter would never enter a department store and think the loudspeaker announcement, 'Welcome Shoppers', referred to her. When she was in prep, we watched TV commercials and I asked her what it was that companies were trying to sell. Even before products appeared on screen, she would answer accurately 'hamburgers', 'cars', 'phones', 'perfume' or 'toys'.

Later, I pushed her further and asked what it was that particular ads were trying to make her *feel*. That question initially took her longer to answer, but soon her responses came as quickly as the ad breaks themselves: 'That I need that toy to be happy... They're saying their hamburgers are great and I'll be happy if I eat one. But they're not that good, Dad, I've eaten them. And they're never that big!'

My campaign to inure her from the evils of consumerism stayed on track through early primary school and eventually she came up with the questions: 'Why do you hate McDonald's so much, Dad?' If she'd been carrying pen and paper, I'd have told her to take notes. Here it is: even though Macca's (how bloody affectionate) had gone health-conscious in recent times, the 100 per cent fat and then some Big Daks, Quarter Pumpers, McNothings and Sundaes (every day of the week, when it comes to chemical ingredients) were still the big sell items. I told her you can't drive from one town to another in this country without seeing a Golden Arch. I asked her what a green road sign meant and she said she didn't know, whereas she had no trouble remembering what the gold one meant. I ranted about the abuse of the environment – a billion burgers worth of beef, to quote my favourite songwriter, Bruce Cockburn – and the 'brazilian' those burgers give Brazilian rainforests (well, I skipped the snip reference). And, in the *pièce de résistance*, I told her they *make* kids work there – and don't pay them a thing.

A few weeks later, Mum picked my daughter up from school and, for a treat, took her to McDonald's. My daughter stopped short in front of the glass doors and looked with concern at her grandmother: 'You're not going to make me work here, are you, Nanny?'

Okay, so I'd pushed it too far. In the ensuing years, I relented and I occasionally took her and her younger brother to McDonald's. I hoped this tactic would prevent a backlash in their twenties when, free of my influence, they might eat burgers and fries for every meal. It seems to have worked; neither of them went crazy, like some of their friends, for fast food.

But, back then at least, my daughter went crazy for shopping – and I felt partly to blame.

◇ ◇ ◇

In July 2009, then US President Barack Obama admitted he hated shopping. What a refreshing piece of information; it could have been twittered to me all year and I wouldn't have deleted it. Whereas our former treasurer, Peter Costello, had once told us we had to shop to keep our economy on track and our own wallets lined, here was the leader of the free world acting free. The bloke hated to shop – and he looked half-decent.

Shopping for Values: A Journey with my Daughter

It was great to know I was in good company whenever I told people I disliked prowling the streets – or the web – especially for clothes. Dads like me and Obama, flat out with work and family, wanted a shop where we could buy in one hour all the clothes we needed for two years, that looked half-way fashionable, without having to try any of them on, without listening to any Top 40 music, and where no one told us we looked good, even if we looked tragic.

But while me and the president could avoid shopping for ourselves, our kids were another story. My daughter's excitement about her Dimmey's debut with Dad had created a monster: she decided her tenth birthday should be a shopping party followed by a sleepover. Her friends' Mums looked at me like I'd lost my trolley. Notwithstanding the fact that I'd have to go shopping at Highpoint (also known by locals as 'No Point') on a Friday night, there was the fact that I'd be doing it with five Year Four girls. 'You're brave', was the popular rejoinder, or a smirk that said, *Good luck, fool*.

My then girlfriend now wife Jo looked at me equally sceptically.

'Is that a good idea?' she winced. She's as anti-consumerist as me and couldn't fathom why I'd take my intelligent, media-savvy tween daughter shopping for her birthday. Wouldn't it undo all I'd been trying to tell her about how brands aren't important and that shopping is a necessity not a hobby?

'Umm, probably', I replied. But when you've seen your daughter's classroom poster – and you've seen also the horror in her eyes the day you had to tell her that her Mum and Dad would never be together again – you make these kinds of concessions. And the shopping trip was okay in the end – we visited Smiggle, where we smelt the fruity erasers, and we skipped through games shops, jewellery outlets, irritating tween girl Top 40 clothes shops and drank stupid amounts of hot chocolate. The girls spent less than ten bucks each and, far from needing brands to impress each other, were happy to buy pens with fluffy feathers. They had a special and unusual night (shopping with a Dad? for a party?) and my daughter kept telling me in private that she loved me. That's worth the tangle of bodies in any megaplex. And it was a one-off.

Umm, no such luck. As part of their dual home arrangement, my kids had a birthday party every second year at my house. For my daughter's twelfth, the roulette wheel spun and landed on me again and, in May '09, she wanted a repeat performance of the *Shopping with Dad Poster Boy Tour '07*. The same wince from my wife and, this time, from me.

'I don't know... Can't you think of something else?'

'But it was fun last time, Dad!'

'Yeah, but –', I said and, as we hit a volleyball over a net in the backyard, I offered her alternatives: a disco, a gymnastics party, a pizza night, an indoor pool party, a picnic, a blah, a blah and a blah.

'The girls loved it too, Dad! They all want to do it.'

My pride swelling, I tried my last weapon: the truth.

'Sweetie, I don't think it's good for you to have a shopping party. Shopping isn't a hobby—'

'—Yes, it is.'

No, it's not, I said, and I gave her all the listen-here-young-lady reasons why it isn't, the main one being that it isn't creative, not like the drawing and writing she liked to do.

'Yes it is, Dad,' she replied, fixing me with one of the most serious expressions I'd seen from her. 'I'm being creative when I look for clothes, when I check out the colours, and I think about the different things I'm going to wear and how they express me', and, she said, *and, and, and,* 'Dad, it's not just *shopping* – we find out about each other cos of what we like and don't like. And we talk and we... hang out'.

She didn't have the words for it, but I knew what she meant: she and her friends bonded when they shopped. Like I'd bonded with her. A week later, she designed an invitation – 'Confessions of a Shop-a-Holic' – and a month later I was at Highpoint with five Grade Six girls, their mouths full of an indistinguishable mix of gum, lollies and Lady Ga Ga lyrics, each arm carrying two shopping bags full of tween jeans, things that smelt 'nice', crap fake gold bracelets, rubber wrist bands (a black one given to me with the word 'strength' written in white) and, I discovered later, in Hannah's shopping bag, Mother's Day and 'Step Mother's Day' presents purchased with money she'd received for her birthday.

That final non-consumerist ring of the cash register thrilled me, but *Shop-a-Holic '09* still gave me pause. Wasn't I, literally and figuratively, shopping for my daughter's love? Yes, she'd bought some presents for her mum and step-mum, but, in allowing my desire to please her to over-ride my values, hadn't I, well, weakened my brand?

An answer came in June of the same year. The kids and I went to the Pompeii Exhibition at the Museum during school holidays; a good old proper, no nonsense excursion: lots of ancient artefacts, paintings of angry Mt Vesuvius, educational 3D movies – and people's tragic deaths described in detail. Afterwards, we ate lunch, quietly thankful that we didn't live near an active volcano. A three-year-old in a cute dress walked past and I felt warmth for her – she wasn't likely to be crushed by falling debris, at least not today. But my daughter's eyes followed her intensely. 'I hate that', she said. 'She doesn't even know what brand she's wearing... Kids don't need brands...'

But my daughter was still wearing mine. I munched my pie in triumph – bring on the teenage years! Well, maybe not bring them on.

2
Dad Radio

I INVENTED 'DAD RADIO' – and its talkback program – to try to get my then seven-year-old son, already as unforthcoming as a teenager, to talk in the car about his school day. The station and its program rated highly. But, as successful as Dad Radio was, it could never have existed without 'Dad Airlines', the business I established more than a decade earlier when the two children from my first marriage were in primary school.

Dad Airlines was the result of my ability to mimic with a cupped hand the tinny sounding announcements flight crews make. You know the ones: 'This is your Captain speaking. We're travelling at seventy thousand feet above woop woop, enjoy your peanuts'. In a desperate effort to settle backseat arguments on long car trips, I chanced upon Dad Airlines and a set of faux tinny cupped hand announcements:

'This is your Captain speaking. I would like to remind you that unruly behaviour when travelling on Dad Airlines could result in a major pocket money fine or the loss of your electronic gadget for a week or longer'.

Or, when aiming to get a trip off to a good start:

'This is your Captain speaking. Thank you for joining us on Flight 22 to Merimbula this morning stopping at Yarragon for lunch and Bairnsdale for dinner and our stopover. If you require any food during the flight, please ask my co-captain, Joanne, and she will provide you with apples and biscuits from her carry bag in the front seat'.

The announcements proved popular and the kids ended up demanding them for any trip to Whereversville. But, as effective as Dad Airlines was in taming the mob, Dad Radio's power to get my then seven-year-old talking really took flight.

I found that the boy, normally only too happy to hum, squeal or sing at any other time of the day or night, was quickly clamming up when asked what was coming up at school or what had been happening. And, because I was then in charge of all drop offs and pick-ups, it made me first detective in charge of extracting this information. But I wasn't getting much more than, 'Nothing', 'I can't remember' or 'Dad, stop asking that', even when I used that Parenting 101 tried-and-true questioning technique: 'So, did/will anything *interesting* happen at school today?'

The boy, however, loved music, mimicking things and generally talking nonsense. So, I brought Dad Radio to the airwaves one morning on a trip to school.

'You're on Dad Radio, the time now is [look at the digital clock the boy loves to read] 8.42 and the temperature outside is [look to the car thermostat) nine degrees...' I would then tell the non-existent listeners I had the boy, a very special guest from his school, in the car studio that morning and I'd welcome him to the talkback program. 'Thanks very much, Dad', the boy would say in his best interviewee voice. 'So, what's coming up there today at school?' I'd ask, and it was incredible the detail I was able to extract when I was a radio announcer: 'Well, today we have computers and I really like computers cos I get

Dad Radio

to do my work, it's numbers and I like numbers, and then I can have free time'.

'And is anything else—' I'd ask, but I often wouldn't get to finish because, though it was bad radio, my guest had a habit of talking over the top of me, telling me what was happening in the playground, what kids were saying, what happened on an excursion and what he might do in drama or Italian.

By the time the interview was over, we were nearly at school. It was time then for the boy to change guises and voices and become an announcer on Dad Radio, a regular on the program who'd run listeners through the morning traffic report. 'Well, Dad, it's banked up on the Westgate (he could see it, just to his right), but everywhere else is running smoothly – and on the train lines, there are delays on the Lilydale, Belgrave and Frankston Lines'. If there was time before we started the daily battle to find a park, he'd burst into a song I'd announce for him, cutting it off mid-lyric perfectly when I stopped the engine. Then he was off and running into the school morning, preparing content for his Drive Time interview later in the day.

3

Anzacism: A Lesson in Civil Religion

MY THEN PREP SON walked towards his school's gymnasium in a line with the rest of his class. It was Friday April 24, 2015 and they were on their way to a special assembly. In his big, broad-brimmed hat, my son was playful and laughing. My wife tried to get his attention with a wave. He saw her but pretended otherwise; he was a cool primary school kid now. Inside, he settled amongst his peers in the front rows, while we wove through a gaggle of kids to the back of the gym. A teacher grabbed a microphone and told the crowd that staff and middle primary school kids had worked hard the last couple of weeks to create what we were about to witness: a celebration of Anzac Day.

In the lead up to the 2015 Anzac Centenary, pundits' use of the word 'celebration' had troubled me, along with what appeared to be the sudden invention of celebratory quilts of poppies. Smiling students now dragged one into view at the front of the gym. Though it wasn't explained during assembly, my son had learnt the connection between the quilts and the red poppy's history, those flowers first to spring from some World War I European battlefields, flowers soldiers had considered soaked in the blood of their fallen comrades. For this member of the audience, it made the sight of smiling students carrying the poppy quilt disturbing.

The student MC told us we were gathered to celebrate the courage, mateship, self-sacrifice and heroic values the Anzacs had demonstrated. There was no mention then, or later, of the horror, futility or violence of war, beyond the numbers (of Australians) killed in them. Whatever history might say, we were told that in World War I, the Anzacs at Gallipoli were fighting for our nation's freedom. As were World War II Anzacs and those in Vietnam. The assembly's set pieces continued and it became clear what we were there to celebrate: an ideal for how people should live, one the Anzac legend exemplified.

'People don't want compulsory religious instruction', my wife said, 'but they let their kids come to this'.

She had a more than full-time job. The only reason she was there was to assess whether the assembly would be a threat to our child's well-being. Now she felt she had the answer.

'Should we pull him out?'

I shrugged. There would be high-level embarrassment for everyone if we marched to the front and escorted our kid from the gym. Neither of us moved. We just stood and listened, though I found myself withdrawing towards the gym's back wall. Another student MC told us who the Anzacs had fought in World War II: 'The Germans, the Italians, the Austrians and the Turks', she said at a great a clip. There was no mention of Australia's relationship with those countries now. I knew two of those races were represented in the assembly hall, but the others may have been. My son was at an age where he saw only good guys and bad guys. Choose your side of the trench and stay there. He was likely to come home and ask, 'Will an Italian shoot me?' It was going to be a fun night of explanation.

The MC moved us onto the Anzac Day Hero Creative Writing Competition. Students had been asked during the week if they had a 'hero' in their family. Now I understood what my son had been on about when we'd walked to the servo to get milk. 'Did Grandpoppy fight in the war?' he asked. 'No', I told him. 'He was too old to go.' I didn't ask what war he meant. The topic had obviously come up at school. And I had the feeling all he'd understood was that Australia wasn't at war now, but had been in 'The War' sometime before he was born. 'Your great-grandfathers both fought in World War II. Your Nanna's Dad fought from 1941 to 1943 in Crete and the Middle East.' I probably gave him this specific detail because Bill's war service had been significant in that side of my family's history. My son said nothing more, but on Thursday brought home from school a piece of butcher's paper covered with crayon-drawn stick figure soldiers and the words, 'My great-grandfather was a hero because he died in the war in 1946'. I smiled. Maybe I shouldn't have. 'Well', I told him, 'your great-grandfather didn't die in the war. He actually died in 1994'. He looked at me strangely. Like I was distorting history.

At the assembly, students won prizes for similar pieces of creative writing about heroes in their families. Not Anzacs in their families. Or soldiers who had died. Or who had returned, maimed or otherwise. Just heroes. My wife turned to me.

'It's just myth-making. I don't want him hearing this', she said, now anxious to find our son's blond head again amongst the mops in the front rows.

'He's probably not taking it in.'

'Maybe. But he'll come home and say *6,000 soldiers died!*'

She was probably right. He loves maths. That he would come home plagued by our joint concern, a religious understanding of what he'd witnessed, seemed less likely. But not impossible. After all, children attend churches, mosques, temples and synagogues every week in Australia. They must be learning something, even if only via osmosis. I wondered if our son was soaking up more than we realised.

It's not a new idea that religious impulses influence the way in which Anzac Day and the Anzacs themselves are commemorated. Weary Dunlop's biographer, Sue Ebury, used the Latin phrase *Via Dolorosa* (Christ's 'way of sorrows' as he carried his cross through Jerusalem) to head one of the chapters on her subject. Stephen Garton, in his essay *War and Masculinity*, noted that there is 'a complex tension between Christian and Classical symbolism' in Australia's war memorials. Ahenk Yilmaz, writing about Gallipoli's war memorials, made the point that even in its infancy the narrative Australia constructed about the events at Gallipoli had the characteristics of a secular religion. He added that civilian Australian and New Zealanders who first visited Gallipoli in 1925, long before interest revived in the 1990s, did so on what were dubbed 'pilgrim ships'.

For secular Australians used to accepting that organised religion is on the wane, it may come as a surprise that, in 'Anzacism', we could be dozily participating in an organised national religion. But it seems Anzacism is one component, likely the strongest, in what Jean-Jacques Rousseau would call Australia's civil religion. As he pointed out in his 18th century work *The Social Contract*, civil religion provides nations with a unifying force. American sociologist Robert Bellah built on Rousseau's initial ideas and suggested that civil religion could include many practices, including adoration bordering on worship for war veterans, and mythologised tales of their deeds and values.

It's not surprising then that *The Australian*'s editor-at-large Paul Kelly, in his analysis of the Anzac centennial commemorations at Gallipoli, spoke of 'Anzac's power' having a 'deeply unifying force'.

The term 'Anzac Spirit' (capitalised like 'Holy Spirit'), invoked to encourage us to live out values dead soldiers are deemed to have embodied *en masse*, is religious language *par excellence*, an oral version of Catholicism's *Lives of the Saints*, one which TV commentators voice in guttural tones during the ANZAC Day football match, and officials voice with a priestly tenor at Dawn Services around the nation and at Gallipoli. Even if we leave aside the religious connotations associated with the blood sacrifice Australians made at Gallipoli, which numerous historians say resulted in our birth as a nation, it seems Manning Clark's notion of Australian religious yearning being 'a shy hope in the heart' doesn't square with Anzacism. It is a bold reality in the public sphere. Former Prime Minister Tony Abbott and the aforementioned Paul Kelly, like zealous prophets, once voiced the importance of our civil religion, the former in his Centenary of Anzac speech at Anzac Cove, the latter in his coverage of the speech and event.

Abbott said we must do more than remember the Anzacs, we must, in Kelly's words, 'emulate their spirit', recalling St Paul's New Testament encouragement for Christians to emulate him as he emulates Christ. The Anzacs, Abbott said, help 'us to be better than we would otherwise be', and Gallipoli, according to Kelly's rendering of Abbott's speech, is about 'perseverance, duty, compassion, conquering fear, and sacrifice for one's friends'. Kelly summed up Australians' duty to emulate theses 'lives of the saints' by saying Abbott's set of values 'invests Anzac with a spiritual essence relevant to any age', before pointing out that the 'originating sacrifice' was 'available from a visit to the beaches, cliffs and the Lone Pine memorial'. As the site of Christ's death is available for Christians who visit Jerusalem.

Our civil religion is powerful and its adherents are furious if it's confronted. SBS journalist Scott McIntyre knows this. Whatever is made of the historical accuracy or moral rectitude of his 2015 Anzac Day tweets, they challenged the official view. His sacking and the virulent responses to his tweets on social media demonstrate that Australia's saints are denigrated at your peril, especially on Anzacism's equivalent of Easter.

◊ ◊ ◊

In the school gymnasium, the recitation of kids' creative writing about heroes finished up. Later, my wife reminded me of the reality behind the man my son had chosen as his hero, a man he'd never met. Bill fought in World War II as a 16-year-old. He lied about his age to get in on the big adventure. He came home wounded and with post-traumatic stress that he tried to self-medicate with alcohol. It didn't work and relatives suffered as a result.

A girl of Vietnamese origin took the microphone and explained that her father fought with the South Vietnamese during the Vietnam War. Although it had been mentioned earlier that the Anzacs had fought alongside him, it was a relief to hear the account of a kid whose hero wasn't an Anzac. Then, a moment of beauty. Perhaps she was the only student in the school who could play the trumpet well enough, but it was fitting that another girl of Vietnamese origin played 'The

Last Post' and we rested our heads with her in the silence that followed.

◊ ◊ ◊

Like many religions, Anzacism has had its periods of decline. After Vietnam and Australia's large anti-war protests, it seemed Anzacism – and Anzac Day – were doomed. But in the early 1990s, as is well-documented, young Australian backpackers began to revive the Anzac Spirit, resuscitating it to life like revivalism is said to do for Christianity.

Alan W. Black said this return to Gallipoli was Australia's foray into a longstanding global tradition of 'international civil religious pilgrimage'. It's likely the backpackers were devoid of traditional religious foundations. Perhaps they also unconsciously sensed that the foundation for life that Australia's civil religion could provide had also waned. In visiting the site of what Kelly called our nation's 'original sacrifice', these young Australians, many the same age as those who had died, were searching for personal meaning. In the process, they put the meaning back into our civil religion. Just in time for the Gulf War, 9/11, Afghanistan and Iraq, the Spirit of Anzac, with John Howard initially cheering it along, could take flesh and march again on battlefields around the globe. Our civil religion then supported not just the spiritual lives of the young, but also the political lives of our leaders. As Paul Kelly said in his paraphrase of Tony Abbott's Gallipoli centenary speech, 'Anzac cannot be static... The story's spiritual dimension is about a stronger and better Australia inspired by the greatness and smallness of what these men did on this shore'. That men and women have been engaged in small and large actions in battle since 9/11 in the ongoing War on Terror means that 'Anzac' (does that oft-used noun denote Australian civil religion's Godhead?) can never be static. Because it is human and fighting around the world, whether we like or not. And if we don't like it, or the civil religion it inspires, then perhaps we best keep quiet if we want to keep our jobs and perhaps some of our friends. Because religious cults, just ask former Scientologists, will cut us off in a heartbeat if we dare cross their holy tenets.

◊ ◊ ◊

The school kids, often boisterous in the ceremony, were remarkably quiet in the aftermath of The Last Post. The Vietnamese girl remained still, head bowed, trumpet at her side. I wished her item had been the only one in the ceremony. That we could simply have listened to her play and lain some wreaths. I'd often thought of my late grandfathers as I'd stood in previous Anzac Day silence. Today, I thought of my friend Khanh. When he was less than half the age of the trumpeter, he'd escaped post-war Vietnam with his father and uncle on a creaky wooden boat. They were lost at sea for weeks. Afraid of pirates. Their boat leaking and young Khanh wondering if he'd ever see his mother again.

The MCs and teachers thanked us for coming and told us the assembly was over. But there were still fifteen minutes before dismissal. Our preppie had to go back to his classroom. I bought some Anzac biscuits from the stall while my wife accompanied him to his room. Later she told me she would likely be dubbed 'the weird mum' from now on. She had met parents outside the classroom who hadn't been to the assembly. A friend of my wife's asked how it had panned out. 'I didn't really like it, actually', she told her. But a number of other parents had said how wonderful it was, the writing, the speeches, and the poppies. My wife went quiet.

In the car on the way home, we asked our son what he thought of it all. What was it about?

'I don't know', he said. We asked him if he understood what had been said about the soldiers, the Anzacs and 'the war'. He squirmed in his car seat, sheepish. He thought he was in trouble.

'I don't know', he repeated. 'I was talking to my friends.'

It's not often, but I'm sometimes glad my son can be just a little disobedient.

4

Heart Prayer

EVERY NIGHT SHE STAYED AT MY HOUSE for five years, I did a prayer for my then thirteen-year-old daughter. And that's not a grammatical error; I did the prayer as much as spoke it.

First, I touched her forehead and said, 'May you think God's thoughts'. Then touched her eyes and ears, asking that she might see through God's eyes and hear how God might want her to live. Then it was her nose: 'May you smell God's wonderful earth'.

I touched her hands and asked that they might be quick to heal, then a quick rub of her tummy: 'May you stomach only what you need to stomach'. And, finally, her favourite part; I touched her on the breastbone, ever so carefully, and said, 'May you love with God's heart, yourself and others'.

When she was younger, she called this ritual the 'God's heart prayer'. Soon, she never went to bed, properly, at my place without me doing it. She told me, too, that sometimes when she was at her mum's place and not feeling in top form, she did our God's heart prayer herself.

She decided eventually that she wanted to live mainly with her mum. There were many reasons. She didn't want to carry her bags as often from house to house; she needed a base; she wanted to connect more with her mum. All fair and reasonable reasons to make a move, and all making me feel like I was losing my daughter, like she was leaving home five years early.

She made her choice after a family therapy session she did with her mother, her brother and me. She said she hoped I would understand. I told her over lunch in a food court that I did and that I loved her and I would be okay. And she saw the tears in my eyes and I'm not sure how confident she was. As part of the therapy, the counsellor asked me privately what things my daughter and I connected around. I told him about the prayer and that she used the prayer at her mum's house.

'She carries it with her', he said. 'She carries you with her.'

I believe that life, from the start, from that moment I looked into my baby daughter's haunting dark eyes, is all about learning to let go. We let go of our cosy womb; we let go of our childhoods, our adulthoods and finally our bodies. We let go of our daughters. Our daughters let go of us. And in that letting go there is death, the death of time I cherished with my daughter, but at the same time new life as she learnt to think her own thoughts, along with God's, without my hand on her forehead as often.

I was sure she would do the God's Heart prayer when she needed to. Like I needed to do it when she left. That I would love with God's heart my daughter, who needed me to set her free.

5

Reality Check

I'M ONE OF EIGHT WESTERNERS standing on a train bridge in 35-degree heat, ready to go on the Dharavi Slum Tour in Mumbai, India. We're huddled together and I don't like it. The train journey here was stuffy and cramped enough, and now I'm about to enter a city within a city, where a million people live and work in just over one and a half square kilometres, half the size of New York's Central Park. I take in the view: a field of rusted tin roofs, piles of plastic chairs, scrap metal, plastic bottles, crumpled olive oil tins, and flags representing the religions that lay claim to its suburbs.

◊ ◊ ◊

I hold my water bottle tight and listen to Majoj, our lanky Gen-Y tour guide. His pep talk includes his bio. He's a student and he wants one day to be a tattoo artist or hairdresser in Switzerland or England, he's not fussy. And he tells us taking photos is banned once we enter the slum.

'If people stare at you, don't worry', Majoj adds, and we walk down the railway bridge into the slum proper. I pathetically slip my hands into my pockets and grip my phone and wallet. I'm not really afraid of losing them. What I'm afraid of losing is their means of escape. As Majoj predicted – and despite these 'Reality Tours' having run twice daily for six years – hundreds of eyes stare at us. They peer from the narrow, bicycle-laden road, from shop doorways, and from behind pushcarts piled high with nylon bags.

The bicycles and pedestrians move more slowly here than in the rest of Mumbai. It's quieter. No beeping black taxis. And no Bollywood billboards or traditionally dressed, Gucci-toting women to distract your eye from the poverty. But, Majoj tells us, while Dharavi may not be rich, it's one of the world's most industrious slums: an annual turnover of about $590 million. And Reality Tours make it their business, literally, to show off this work, guiding Westerners through the plastic and aluminium recycling, pottery, embroidery, baking, soap-making, leather tanning and pappadum-making.

Majoj leads us into a tiny, airless 'warehouse' where five bare-chested men liquefy recycled metal in two exposed furnaces, slightly larger but decaying versions of household wood heaters. The heat is intense from ten metres away, but these guys are almost in the flames – and without any protective clothing. Majoj says they don't wear it because it slows their work rate and potential income.

'They work 70 hours a week', Majoj says, adding that they earn about $90 per month, just enough to survive. 'Some also sleep there to give free security for the factory owners.' He says this is a decent living in a tight-knit and supportive community.

We wend for ages through a laneway devoid of daylight, with the walls and concrete path caked in a black viscous substance – what appears to be a combination of oil and mud. Water runs along drainage ruts that I carefully step around. There are one-room homes cut into walls, where several people squat on concrete floors. And all around us, whether in laneways or on the rooftops, there's rubbish. Dharavi is a garbage tip interrupted by buildings and people, but I can't throw away my now empty plastic water bottle. I want to ask Majoj if there's a bin somewhere, see if he gets my attempt at humour, but I stop myself. I keep hold of the bottle, grip it like a staff.

We enter a building that has neither name nor purpose, just a thoroughfare between our last patch of sunlight and the plastics recycling plant to which we're headed. Inside, people ferret in rags, smells rise up that I can't identify, but are strong enough to make me gag. Heat closes in and there's not enough room to swing one of the stalking cats.

The experience is disorientating. Where's this tour going? What are these people on about?

We reach the plastics recycling control centre. It's a tight space that could be an office, or a museum exhibit of one. There's a dusty desk and a cupboard. On top of some empty hessian bags lies a sleeping man. Majoj ignores him and talks loudly about the tiny yellow pellets in a small cardboard box on the desk. These are the end result of the recycling activity that is, we're assured, taking place around us, even if we can't see it. The towers of plastic bottles, the millions of plastic containers, are recycled into these pellets and sold back to the Chinese. They become a whole new batch of plastic bottles and containers.

We leave and walk in sunlight for a blessed ten minutes. I feel strangely liberated and I throw my water bottle away, add to the hundreds around me, feeling that in doing so I've participated in Dharavi's life. In the residential area now, I observe the slow progress of a thin, grey river. It carries the smell of excrement, rubbish and animal remains into the

Arabian Sea. But people smile, kids laugh – and they chase us, just to touch us, and, unlike in other parts of Mumbai, no one begs. The kids, we're told, would be in school uniforms if it were a weekday. Majoj says many business people who could live elsewhere choose to remain with their families in Dharavi. 'It's their home', he says.

A dirt-floored alcove where a tall man with grey hair in a heavy black apron tans and cuts leather. Men panel beat used industrial-sized olive oil tins until they're shiny enough to go back into the market. If the tins are too far-gone, women sit in the dirt and tear them apart for later use as building material. Later, we see a Mumbai staple: an impromptu cricket match on stony ground.

Beyond the cricket there's a set of speakers and people dancing to a techno beat on a mound of earth. I wouldn't have described the atmosphere in Dharavi up until that point as gloomy, but it was definitely sober. Now there's a carnival in progress: old and young rumble and shake and dance as if in one of Mumbai's nightclubs.

Majoj chooses this funky moment to inform us that almost a third of the slum's residents don't have access to a toilet. And then there are those who don't bother using the ones available because the queues are so long. Human waste, I'm told, is likely to be that merry dance floor's foundation.

He takes us to a courtyard edged by drains carrying filthy water. Women put pappadums out to dry in the sun where flies quickly swarm them. We enter a house only a little larger than my bathroom; Reality Tours rents it to show Dharavi's average living conditions. A family of at least five would normally occupy this space, which has what I take to be thick shelving on the walls, but I learn are sleeping slots. There's also a table, a water jug and a light bulb. A family pays $35 per month to live here, which takes most of their wages.

Our tour continues with a stroll through the pottery industry, an area so thick with smoke from primitive kilns that I cough all the way to our second-last stop: a community centre and kindergarten that Reality Tours built. It's Saturday so the buildings are empty, but noticeboards, kids' games and furniture give evidence this is all bona fide. I've been trying to catch Reality Tours out the whole time, cynically hoping they were ripping off the locals so I could dob them in. To whom, I'm not sure.

We're ushered to Reality Tours' office. We can buy postcards, or catch our breath, or have a Coke or bottled water (yes, more recycling). We pay our fee and give our tour guide his tips. I put a ten-rupee note in an envelope for Majoj and hope it's some help for his tattooing or hairdressing dreams. For once, the image of Gandhi on the note doesn't seem out of place. Even if I do.

Back at my hotel, my feet are sore. My clothes smell of kiln smoke and my boots are covered in dust. But I'm strangely energised; enlarged yet humbled. When I talk to others about the tour, I can't shut up about it: the fear, the exposure to a world I didn't know existed, the industry, the men as zoo exhibits, the filth, the smiling kids. Should these other potential visitors go? If they'd asked me a few days later, after I'd seen an elderly couple living with dog-sized rats in an abandoned yard near our hotel, I'm not sure what I would have said. That couple's ragged faces made me think that any attempt to alleviate extreme poverty was doomed. But today, still inspired, I don't hesitate: 'Yes, you should go on the slum tour'. And the next day, five more Westerners are on a cramped and sweaty train to Dharavi.

6

Father's Day Music Club

IN THE LEAD UP TO FATHER'S DAY, my twenty-year-old son gave me one of the best gifts a man my age could get: an invitation to join his exclusive online music appreciation group.

Along with him and his COVID-19, locked-down millennial buddies, I got to add to the group playlist the songs and albums that had made my life. 'Because, Dad', he messaged me, 'we're listening to a lot of old stuff at the moment'.

For them, that meant Nirvana, The Smiths, Joy Division and Smashing Pumpkins. I developed immediate posting paralysis, worried I'd suggest an album that would embarrass me.

'How do I do this, son? Can I just anonymously stick something on there?' No, what I had to do was type a little intro into the Messenger group then post a link to a song or album.

So, I tried: 'Teenage Fanclub, band that supported Nirvana in early '90s and Cobain described as the best in the world. I like to imagine Kurt standing beside the stage listening to 'The Concept' and just gaping in amazement'.

And I sent them a link to the Scottish outfit's 1991 album, *Bandwagonesque*. I received *four* love heart reactions, plus some welcomes to the group.

I got my Father's Day present because I'd finally caught the beat – my son wanted to connect with me through music. I'd been fretting about how to maintain a relationship with him – a young adult in a share house during COVID-19 – while he was sending me messages about the music he was listening to in lockdown. And I kept bouncing messages back: 'great album' or 'nice track'. Instead of going deep.

The deep conversation started when he messaged me asking if I had a favourite Joy Division song. I came straight back with 'Love Will Tear Us Apart'. He responded with the laugh-'til-you-cry emoji and 'Come on, branch out a little!' The trouble was, I couldn't. As much as I knew Joy Division were seminal, cool, tragic, luminescent and every other alt rock cliché, I hadn't listened to them much. And I decided to risk telling my son why.

In the early '90s, there was a recession on, just like today. I couldn't get a job after finishing my journalism degree, so I fudged my way into working as a nurse's assistant at a nursing home. I was alone after midnight in the Alzheimer's ward, silent but for the occasional murmur from a sleeping resident. I patrolled eerie corridors and, when I came to the dark lounge room, a TV was playing *Rage* at low volume. I hunched in close, listened to mournful singing and synth sounds, watched cloaked figures in black and white carry large photographs of people through a desert scape. And I got the chills.

I found out later it was the 1980 film clip to Joy Division's 'Atmosphere', but as I watched it then, I knew I couldn't listen to that band. Struggling with mental health issues that remain never far from view, it felt to me that Joy Division could soundtrack me to a place I didn't want to go.

I explained all this to my son.

'well that was far more than i bargained for hahahah but that is actually extremely interesting to hear' he messaged back.

It got us chatting about deep stuff, things we normally wouldn't find a way to discuss, especially the impact of mental health on lives and careers. The music appreciation group my son had started was one way he was trying to help keep his friends' spirits up. They were all nearing the end of their university degrees and heading into one of the most uncertain job markets in Australia's history.

But that conversation was for another day. He wanted to know what Velvet Underground I'd listened to.

7

Taking the Poison out of Masculinity

A DOWNY COVERING of blond hair had grown on his shins. My youngest son was growing up. He was trying to push back his bedtime and, when it was my turn to try to get him down for the night, I opted for a strict routine. I lay next to him and read from a *Speccy Magee* book he'd already read (he liked the voices I put on), then prayed with him. The latter involved what he called our 'normal prayer', which was repeat of the 'heart prayer' I'd done with my daughter, gently touching his stomach, arms, legs, lips, head and chest, and announcing how each might be inhabited, sanctified, if you like, by God. Then came our 'special prayer', which was largely me speaking aloud the good things I hoped life would hold for him. I usually closed proceedings by saying, 'Goodnight, beautiful boy'.

Until one night. Instead of saying goodnight back, he admonished me.

'Boys can't be beautiful!'

I shouldn't have been surprised at that remark. He was, after all, growing up; fairytales were no longer his books of choice, and he was putting Santa's purported ability to visit several billion homes in one night through his burgeoning maths skills.

'Yes, they can be beautiful. Inside and out.'

He didn't reply so perhaps my answer satisfied him. But his silence might also have meant, *Are you crazy, Dad?*

Between birth and about three years old, while they're mewling on bunny rugs and crawling for soft toys, it's acceptable to dub boys 'beautiful'. Then it all changes soon after school starts; if parents, relatives and friends still describe boys as beautiful, it generally isn't within their earshot. Boys might get embarrassed: *I'm not beautiful! I'm... I'm...* on their way to being tweens, teenagers and then young adults. Our boys might grow up, but the idea of themselves as beautiful, if they ever had it, goes down, into the depths of their souls and psyches. Even in this more gender-enlightened age, many boys get the strong message from peers and other parts of our culture that inner and outer beauty is feminine. And femininity is still too often associated with weakness. Boys can't show themselves as vulnerable or in need of emotional comfort. They hear that they need to be strong. Toughen up, princess!

Still, their beauty won't disappear. It can't. Because it's from the One who made them, who wants that beauty to be revealed to the world.

At least some of people's unwillingness to dub boys of a certain age 'beautiful' is no doubt the result of not wanting to appear connected with the scourge of paeodophilia. It may mean even parents are unwilling to describe their young sons as beautiful, but it doesn't have to mean avoiding *thinking* they're beautiful, and treating them that way.

We want men whose masculinity ensures they treat women with respect and kindness, while understanding that women and men are inherently equal. But, attempts by corporations like Gillette aside, it remains less acceptable for males to treat other males gently and kindly than it is acceptable for women to so treat them. Because boys are not taught to honour themselves, their bodies, emotions and spirits. They're not taught that they're beautiful, inside and out.

In *Healing Through the Dark Emotions*, psychotherapist Miriam Greenspan argues that western culture largely won't accept that wisdom can be gained by living through – instead of subjugating – three big and so-called 'dark' emotions: grief, despair and fear. 'A culture that insists on labelling suffering as pathology', she writes, 'that is ashamed of suffering as a sign of failure or inadequacy, a culture bent on the quick fix for emotional pain, inevitably ends up denying both the social and spiritual dimensions of our sorrows.'

Of those three big, dark emotions, fear is arguably the one that boys (and men) are taught has no place in their masculine identities. To show fear is to appear weak. But, according to Greenspan, denial of fear is the root of many serious psychological issues.

'When we don't know the contours of our fear, when we can't experience it authentically or speak about it openly, we are more likely to be afflicted with anxieties and phobias, panic, obsessive-compulsion, psychosomatic ills, and all kinds of controlling, destructive, and violent behaviours.'

The last three on Greenspan's list, especially, read as a check-list for the behaviours inherent to what has been described as 'toxic masculinity'. I've come to realise that if I want my son to avoid this and retain his sense of being beautiful – and to grow into a beautiful man – I have to help him express and live with fear, not help him deny it or simply 'manfully' conquer it.

It's not a stretch to believe, either, that Christianity has had an impact upon men seeing fear as something to deny. After all, Jesus spends a lot of time reportedly telling believers to 'fear not'. But he *doesn't* say there's nothing to fear. Only that he has overcome the worst the world can do to us. And Jesus had no problem expressing his own fear, namely in the Garden of Gethsemane as he sweated blood fearing his execution, nor did he struggle to express his grief and despair.

My son was scared of storms, spiders, bullies, aggressive dogs and being away from his parents for more than two nights. The change in him when I told him his fear was normal and okay was phenomenal. He gained peace of mind when I told him that what was happening in his body, the tears, the tremors, the clenching in his stomach, was natural and okay, too.

He began to accept fear as part of life, not something to shun, but something he could learn from as he listened to what his body and mind were telling him. Fear doesn't feel beautiful, but accepting it will mean he's less likely to grow ugly inside and act out destructively.

I overheard a conversation he instigated with three boys, one the same age as him, and two who were older. He asked them, 'Are you guys scared of anything?' The other boys froze. What should they say? If they admitted to being fearful, wasn't that going against some unwritten rule? After a while, the eldest said he was scared of a particular breed of dog. His relief at having got it out was palpable, and it released the rest of the boys to confess that, yes, they were scared of some things, too.

The truth and freedom. Helping boys admit their fear and teaching them to live with it is only one way to help them stay beautiful and grow into beautiful men. But in a culture decrying a crisis in masculinity, it's a simple approach that might have a long-term impact on making our world a place where women feel safe – because men feel safe in themselves.

8

Ripe for the Picking

WE WERE THE LOQUAT HOUSE. Every spring when the fruit ripened on the tree in our front yard, elderly suited Greek men and widows in black dresses appeared on our doorstep, asking if they could fill empty shopping bags with this strange, bitter crop. Glad to be rid of the fruit, I told them to get stuck into it and they went to work on the low branches. I helped by climbing a stepladder and plucking the yellow perils from the upper limbs.

I'd never heard of loquats before moving into our rental house in Kingsville. But I soon found out they were the first of the summer stone fruits to ripen, they were native to south-eastern China, took off to Japan about a thousand years ago, then migrated to the sub-continent. They later spread throughout the Mediterranean basin, hence the visits from our Greek friends, who told me they used them in fruit salads, jams and chutneys. Loquats were too tart for my family's taste, but I'm glad they found their way to local jars and bowls.

During summer, branches hung heavy with fruit over fences in many Kingsville laneways. Our family's dusk walks saw us return with the bottom of the pusher full of peaches, plums, apricots, figs, pomegranates and even passionfruit. Herbs were bountiful and, of course, lemons. It was amazing how much food you could get by picking what was hanging in the suburb, or by going the extra step and asking neighbours if you could have some of their surplus.

We were gleaners, but minor players compared to Jonathan and Kim Cornford, who then lived in Footscray. Jonathan has a PhD in international development, and had studied and worked in the Mekong delta, assessing poverty in southwest Vietnam. Kim had put her honours degree in economics to work in poverty-stricken Laos and with marginalised people in Melbourne. The couple run a not-for-profit organisation called Manna Gum, which educates churches and other faith organisations about what the Judeo-Christian tradition says about economics.

'We run popular education around understanding how the ways in which we live contribute to outcomes in poverty, understanding that link', Jonathan said, adding that people talked a lot about the planet's health. 'We ask what health "looks" like when it comes to our neighbours, the community and the earth.'

For the Cornfords, it looked like a backyard full of chooks and fruit trees, a thriving vegetable patch, including homegrown garlic and herbs, and a bee hive on the garage roof. Gleaning the local neighbourhood for food was a logical next step for them. And they had a systematic, seasonal and multi-box approach to harvesting the suburb.

'We get boxes of apricots, peaches, plums and, of course, lemons', Kim said. 'But we also get feijoas, figs, almonds, apples...'

Through gleaning, the Cornfords were almost self-sustaining in fruit. They made their own cordial, preserved dozens of fruits, made a dessert to die for called Figs in Port, even lollies from lemon rind. They joined with teams of other neighbourhood gleaners and visited local trees according to the season, boxes in hand, and the neighbours knew they were coming.

The Cornfords had strong relationships in the community and networked with other gleaners citywide. They swapped each other's harvests, meaning the couple had scored cherries and nashi pears from over east. And Feral Fruit Trees Melbourne, a website Axel White created, marked the trees that were ready to glean. He said there were plenty of international fruit tree maps online, but none in Australia.

'I was out riding my bike with a friend during autumn while there were a lot of trees fruiting at the time, and mentioned how great it would be to map them all out and do a big harvest.'

Axel got back on his bike and plotted the fruiting trees in the Brunswick area that were outside the boundary of private property, or had branches hanging over a fence.

'Suburban fruit picking is an old idea, kids have always done it. Of course, it's getting a lot more attention now because of a growing concern for the environment', he said, adding that he encouraged gleaners to always ask owners if it was okay to take fruit, even if it was hanging in public spaces.

Jonathan and Kim found that, even after swapping with fellow gleaners, they had leftovers, which they donated to the food co-op to which they belonged, to other families, and to the poor.

'We don't consider ourselves poor, although we are statistically on the low-income scale', Jonathan said, 'but gleaning had an economic impact for us. And, for people struggling to put together a food budget, gleaning certainly could be significant'.

For the Cornfords, neighbourhood gleaning had its basis in ancient Jewish rural economic practices. The Torah, especially the books of Deuteronomy and Leviticus, referred to them, with Leviticus saying, 'When you reap the harvest of your land, do not reap to the very edges of your field or gather the gleanings of your harvest. Leave them for the poor and the alien'.

Refugees and the poor could gather (glean) the leftovers, what farmers didn't – or couldn't – harvest. The later rabbinical writers said farmers shouldn't benefit from gleanings, and weren't allowed to discriminate among the poor or frighten them away with dogs or lions. The gleaning idea spread to Europe, evidenced by 19th Century French artworks, particularly Jean-François Millet's famous *Des Glaneuses* (1857). In 19th century England, gleaning was a legal right for 'cottagers', farm labourers who didn't own land.

Today, the Slow Movement defines gleaning as groups collecting crops from fields that have been mechanically harvested, or fields where, due to low market prices, it's not economically profitable to harvest. It doesn't talk about neighbourhood gleaning, but says farm gleaning is one of a number of 'food recovery' processes, including salvage from restaurants, that help feed today's poor.

The Society of St Andrew in the US is entirely dedicated to feeding the poor through gleaning, its volunteers gathering leftover fruit and vegetables from fields. Faith Feeds in Kentucky has a similar ethic, as does Island Grown, an organisation based on Martha's Vineyard, an island off the coast of Massachusetts. Table to Table in Israel, following the biblical edict, also institutes gleaning as part of its wider program of food redistribution. And, while they don't feed the poor, New England's The Three Foragers explain on their blog how to collect and cook the food growing wild on their doorstep. However, apart from Greek and Italian Australians continuing the practice in the suburbs, the ancient custom of gleaning hasn't gained much traction here.

'The Hebrew Bible has numerous laws around food waste and the surplus economy,' Jonathan said. 'The Torah has an economic vision at its heart and it's based on there being such a thing as too much and certainly such a thing as too little. The "promised land" is a place where everyone has enough'.

The ancient Hebrews also had a challenging notion of property rights, claiming that beyond a certain point personal property belonged to the community. 'There was a stakehold in your property that the rest of the community had, particularly the poor.'

So, taking an ancient Middle Eastern perspective, that peach I had just picked from my neighbour's tree belonged to me anyway. Perhaps this was instinctive knowledge, and why neighbours were happy to give away their excess.

'The Torah has laws which, to us, across the chasm of history and geography, seem bizarre. But, actually, they are the outworking of a vision of enough for everyone and ecological care.'

9

Cuisines of the World and Crazy Thursday

EVERY FORTNIGHT, my two primary-school-aged kids from my first marriage came to me and my wife for one night. Crazy Thursday. Then they went back to their mum for a week.

It was impossible, in fact it felt stupid, to try to carry on a normal family routine on Crazy Thursday. The kids were disrupted and out of sorts, but the arrangement was at that time set in something stronger than stone: court orders.

I felt out of sorts, too. Melancholy because I knew they were only with me for one night and then they'd be gone for a week. And, because the kids were unhappy, I was plagued by a sense of failure. I explained the situation to a family counsellor that my wife and I were seeing at the time and he agreed change was needed.

'You've got to find a way to make that night special', he said.

Turn Crazy Thursday into *Happy* Thursday? Sounded good, but how? Play Twister in our PJs? Not known for my light bulb moments, one nevertheless floated above my head like an aroma from a fine dining kitchen.

'Like take them out to dinner?'

Can't pretend it's a normal family night then. But the kids were fussy eaters and were new to my wife's cooking, which was a hundred steps up from my then best effort of packet Mexican. Still, they did at least politely turn up their noses at beautifully prepared broccoli, sweet potato, cous cous, lentils, salmon, red peppers, osso buco and Niçoise salad.

'Let's go out for dinner to a different country's cuisine every Crazy Thursday. Call it *Cuisines of the World*', my wife said.

Now, that was a light bulb.

We lived in the inner west and our trial first destination was West Footscray's Aangan Indian Restaurant. Known as a curry, ah, hotspot, it was bound to stretch the kids' palates. In the courtyard on a balmy November night, my older son quickly found on the menu a facsimile of his favourite dish: fried chicken. It was 'Tawa Chicken', the ingredients described as cooked together (i.e. fried) on a griddle. He loved it. But he didn't stop there, also having a go at Aloo Palak, a vegetarian number (45 to be precise) that included a food he'd never eaten: spinach. And it wasn't even fried.

'Where can we go next time, Dad?' he beamed as I handed over the cash. Hmmm, I'd fed the family for under $110. Crazy Thursday had turned its insanity to my wallet. I wanted to answer by saying we'd go English, the fish and chip shop, but I spun the globe in my mind and stuck the pin on Japan.

My son found fried chicken easy enough on the menu at Matsumoto Japanese Restaurant in East Brunswick. But after JFC, he moved onto chicken in nori rolls, and even had a go at some sushi.

Cuisines of the World and Crazy Thursday

It was expensive, but this antidote to Crazy Thursday was working. The kids were trying new foods, getting to stay up late, and we were all having fun. Especially trying to come up with reasonably priced, authentic world cuisine. The kids pushed for French, I took out a loan, but then my wife suggested the former Café Breizoz in Williamstown. Brittany-inspired, its galettes and crepes were close enough to my daughter's favourite food, pancakes. My son graduated to fried quail at Star Vietnamese Restaurant in Footscray, and we all tried fish direct from the tank. My daughter dipped into guacamole at Tres Tacos in Flemington, the boys found meatlovers paradise at Pireaus Blues Greek in Fitzroy, and my eldest son couldn't find anything fried on the Injera bread at Kensington's The Abyssinian.

My highlight came at Patee Thai in Fitzroy. Except for TV dinners, the kids had never gone floorside to eat. They smiled at each other, trying to figure out how to sit, but clearly impressed with how experimental they were. They tucked into Thai Fish Cakes, savouring the salmon they'd spat out a few months earlier. Asian Greens were no obstacle, and neither were Garlic Chive Dumplings, Vegetarian Green Curry Puffs or Calamari with Chilli and Basil.

I sipped my beer, knowing the night was going to make me another $100+ lighter, but feeling a whole lot lighter in myself. Crazy Thursday had become my favourite night of the fortnight.

The kids' care arrangements, thankfully, changed. There were no more Crazy Thursdays. My wife and I also had a new baby who liked to eat in. Every night. But Cuisines of the World rolled on. The kids devoured my wife's cooking, her splashes of the Mediterranean, and I cooked more, 'specialising' in Asian and Italian. Even better, the kids now cooked. While many their age were inspired by TV's *Junior Master Chef*, I knew my kids' forays into Chinese and Thai cooking was a product of how we fried old Crazy Thursday.

10

Two Bobs' Worth

IN THE BLACK AND WHITE PHOTO, my father Bob and his best friend, Bob Day, are both wearing white singlets and striped bathing trunks, standing on a beach in front of a cobblestone retaining wall. They hold cricket stumps aloft in mock battle poses while their wives, Barb and my mum Carol, sit on towels in modest floral bikinis, feigning damsels in distress.

I loved that photo growing up. It made me want to have lifelong friends. Bob Day, a tall man, mainly torso, towers over Dad, his 'little mate'. Though the pair are play fighting, there's a protectiveness about the taller Bob's gaze through his horn-rimmed glasses, as if he has my father's back. I imagine that's how it was when they went to school together in Hamilton, when they played cricket together, and when they worked as bank tellers in their early twenties; big Bob looking out for his smaller mate. I know it's true of how they played tennis together in a team Bob Day formed in the 1980s. The home court was on Bob Day's sprawling Ocean Grove property, and big Bob would waddle the baselines like a giant seagull, cleaning up anything his little mate missed on the net.

When the beach photo was taken, the two Bobs had already known each other fifteen years. But their play fight was an omen of later friction; Bob Day developed an aspirational lifestyle and began to mock my folks' conservatism. By 2004, fifty years after they'd met, the two Bobs were still living in Geelong, but no longer in contact. Five years later, they parted geographically, too, when Bob Day left Geelong to spend the next eleven years in Loddon Prison, Castlemaine.

◊ ◊ ◊

Dad spent the first few years of his retirement impersonating that figure of ridicule from advertising campaigns: the retired man who doesn't know what to do with himself and is derided for getting in his wife's way. In order to stay clear of Mum – and because golf was off limits due to a back injury – Dad booked a daily seat in front of his widescreen TV. He bet small on big races, and he read the newspaper. He propped himself on ergonomic cushions and commentated on Geelong Football Club and the evils of the AFL's management of his beloved game.

'I don't know what to do about your father', mum said when I visited. She's a five-foot-one, red-haired firebrand.

'Take him out the back and shoot him.'

'I don't need jokes.'

'Yeah, I know. It would mess up the flower bed.'

She sighed and took the wooden spoon out of the cake mix.

'He's hopeless.'

'What about volunteer work?'

'Oh, he's too lazy to be bothered with that now.'

My parents went to counselling. I'm not privy to the details, but afterwards Dad started to regain some of his, you wouldn't say *mojo*, but you might say *heave-ho*. He got off his lounge chair more often. And he became a volunteer loan consultant with the Geelong branch of No Interest Loan Scheme (NILS). The group, as the title suggests, offers people from lower socio-economic backgrounds no interest loans for essential items.

'Well, at least he's doing *something*', Mum said. 'But he won't use his hearing aid.'

◊ ◊ ◊

I don't know when I met Bob Day. It's like trying to remember when I met Dad. The loud, jolly, brattish and opinionated man was always part of my life. He was there when I was an eighteen-month-old in nappies the day of that beach photo. He drank stubbies at my twenty-first birthday party and again at my first wedding three years later.

In the '80s, Bob and family lived in Woodlands, an aptly named area of Ocean Grove. On tennis match day, we drove past plenty of large blocks to get to their place and my brothers and I would look for the odd ones out.

'That one', I'd say, pointing to a block covered with trees, but Mum would always chip in, Buddha-like, 'Just because you can't see the pool or the tennis court, doesn't mean it's not there'.

Doctors, lawyers, business owners and league footballers lived in Woodlands. Ken Dew, owner of Candy's Goldmine, Geelong's discount clothes empire, lived behind Bob's tennis court, while champion Geelong footballer Mick Turner lived next-door. During summer, Mick often came over for a beer and watched the last set of tennis.

'Nice shot, Daisy', he'd encourage his neighbour from a folding chair.

Bob Day was a decent player, but it wasn't until the match was over that he really held court.

'Now, who needs another beer?'

He'd hand them around, with his life wisdom.

'Nothing good comes out of Horsham, everyone knows that, Carol.'

It was Mum's hometown. She'd half scowl, half smile at him.

'Oh, shut up, Day. You're from bloody Branxholme!'

But Bob Day read books my Mum and Dad had never heard of and he'd obviously made something of his life. You only had to look at his five-bedroom house, the tennis court, the caravan, and the gardens. He ran a business called Grove Conveyancing, with an office in Geelong's CBD.

'That's enough from the office lady.'

'Well, you're a bloody conveyance clerk. You only *work* in a lawyer's office!'

Bob Day shared his premises with a lawyer, Philip Boston. Dad attended some of Boston and Day's extensive Friday lunches. After Bob went to prison, Dad said Friday wasn't their only big lunch day.

Mum was always making Bob Day aware that he wasn't a lawyer, but whatever she said never bothered him. It was as if she were relating a fairytale and he was tolerating it. And Dad never joined in to attack Bob, even when Bob Day had a dig at him. But Dad joined in the drinking. Mum drove us home from Ocean Grove to Belmont one night after a big tennis win. Dad had tried to keep pace with Bob Day and some equally sizable teammates and, when we pulled into the driveway, Dad shot from the front seat to throw up on the lawn.

'That's what you get for drinking with the big boys', Mum scolded him.

◊ ◊ ◊

Bob Day became an even bigger boy. He moved from Woodlands to the exclusive Geelong suburb of Newtown, into another sprawling ranch, this one worth a lot more. 'How's he doing that as a conveyance clerk?' Mum would spit, but Dad, as always, wouldn't reply.

At our social gatherings, Bob Day's attack on my parents' conservatism continued. Then there was the fact that Dad didn't work for himself, that Dad, a bank manager, was a 'puppet for the man'.

Bob appeared vindicated when Dad was retrenched in Geelong's recession of the early '90s. He ended up working at a petrol station as a console operator, my first job when I started uni. At later social gatherings, Bob and Barb were still around, but though they were still in the centre of the action, it felt to me they were distant. I wouldn't have said above everyone, but others might have.

By the early noughties, Dad had accepted, without animosity, that his friendship with Bob was fading, but Mum was put out. She didn't like to be considered beneath anyone. She'd talk with Barb on the phone from time to time, as Dad did too when the rumour started that Jeff Day, Bob's cousin and bookkeeper, had stolen cheques from Grove Conveyancing to fund a gambling addiction.

Worse was to come for Barb. When she was on holidays with her husband in London in 2004, Bob Day was phoned and told Grove Conveyancing had collapsed. The newspapers reported that he'd made 'two desperate attempts' to keep the business afloat, both of which had failed. Investigations began immediately, which led police to want to chat with Bob. Barb returned home, but Bob decided to remain in the UK. It seemed he didn't want the holiday to end.

Mum and Dad talked to Barb on her return.

'I don't know why they want to talk to him, Carol,' she said. 'And why now? It's a very difficult time for us.' She had no inkling then that her husband had over fifteen years stolen seven million dollars of his clients' money. Some of those clients were elderly, others disabled. Many were trusted friends.

Bob Day had used his wit and charm to encourage people to invest with him, and had then used their money to cover his investment debts, interest charges, and his credit cards and lifestyle. Which included putting his kids through exclusive private schools.

He came out of hiding and surrendered to police in May 2008. He entered the Geelong police station with a newspaper covering his face, but popped his head up for some typical Bob Day bravado.

'Couldn't you have found better things to do this morning?', he asked the paparazzi. Doubtless those whom Bob owed money thought the media were in the right place at the right time. Especially wheelchair-bound widow Mavis Avery. Bob owed her $414,000, her life savings.

'I only ever met the man once and he told me he'd look after me. He did know that I lost two dear family members', she told the *Geelong Advertiser*.

Bob also knew she had a terminal tumour and that she wanted to leave something for her daughters. But Mavis and hundreds of others will probably never see their money again: there was only $200,000 in Grove Conveyancing's trust account at the time of its collapse. Police investigations never located the rest of the money, and most of Day's former investors believe Bob has hidden it in overseas accounts to access when he's released from jail. Justice Forrest, who sentenced Bob, told the *Herald-Sun* that a forensic accountant had spent several years trying to piece together Bob's financial affairs, detailed on 'scrappy pieces of paper', adding that '[t]he paper trail cannot be followed as such because of the lack of paper'.

When Bob was tried and sentenced, I tried to talk to Dad about it.

'What do you think of it all?' I asked Dad as he tended sausages on his electronic barbecue.

'Not much.'

'He was your mate.'

'Well, people make their choices.'

'How do you feel about it?'

'I don't really want to talk about it at the moment.'

'He was your best friend.'

Dad turned the sausages. Case closed.

He might have been worried someone would come knocking on his door, asking for money. But his silence may also have been because he simply didn't need to say anything because the facts spoke for themselves.

And they continued to. Mum was in touch with Barb during Bob's sentencing.

'He says he's innocent.'

When I contacted Bob in jail, he didn't want to chat. But he wrote me a letter, the details of which he didn't want me to reveal. There was no talk in the letter about his guilt or innocence. Just disappointment that no one had come to visit him.

◊ ◊ ◊

Dad lost thousands in the Pyramid collapse in the early '90s – and his job when Geelong Building Society went down with it – but he didn't go down with Bob Day. There was never a chance of it. After all, Dad was too conservative.

'Robert Day may have stolen Mum's money', Mavis Avery's daughter Linda wrote in *That's Life* magazine, 'but she has something he'll never have – the right to hold her head high, knowing she's a good and honest person'.

Bob Day likes to read widely and may happen across this piece. Perhaps he will dispute his portrait. Dad might dispute it, too. And his own. It's also pointless to consider one human being's worth beside another's. Bob Day will always be worth more to Barb than a truckload of Bob Mitchells. Just as Dad is worth more to me than a few million Bob Days. But the facts are plain: Bob Day's reputation was destroyed and he went lonely to a provincial prison. Dad scaled down his house to an apartment, but he had his liberty. His plants produced good tomatoes, he had time to fish and travel with his wife and sons, and time to get to know his grandchildren. And he still volunteered helping the poor, disabled and elderly get fridges and washing machines.

'Why doesn't your father use his hearing aid?' Mum asked me when I visited. I didn't reply. But it might be a case of Dad hearing no evil so he didn't have to speak any.

11

Play it Again. This Time with Feeling

WHEN HE TURNED THREE, my youngest son collapsed in tears on the lounge room floor beside his birthday present, a new Casio keyboard. My wife and I thought, *Oh, no, another tantrum...* 'What's the matter?' she asked. 'I don't know,' he sobbed. The keyboard's play-along version of Greensleeves tinkered on. 'Are you all right?' she asked again. 'I'm sad!' he said, unable to haul himself from the floor.

In the kitchen later, he hummed Greensleeves and started bawling. We were convinced then we'd found the source of his disturbance: a four-hundred and thirty year-year-old English folk song.

The next day, he wanted to play with his keyboard again. He was excited. And happy. But as soon as he flicked the switch to Greensleeves, he cried. In fact, he became listless and inconsolable. And we had to use high-level diversionary tactics (ice-cream) to stop him from humming the song.

He's always loved music and could even then hum complex melodies seconds after hearing them. At three, he sat through an hour of Dad butchering his acoustic guitar and singing Neil Young. He definitely loved a tune. Perhaps too much.

Play it Again. This Time with Feeling

It's obvious music can affect mood. We've all experienced it. Listen to Slayer or Mozart's *Requiem* and you're sure to spiral down. Likewise, the cheery swell of the third movement of Vivaldi's *Spring* makes us swing from the trees. But it seems odd that *any* music could have had a three-year-old drowning his Casio in tears.

We had dinner with a friend, a career musician. He said it was impossible that the music had incited our son's tears. 'There has to be some other trigger to make that happen.' Jo and I were concerned. Depression runs in both our families.

I found some parents online whose toddlers had experienced tearful responses to 'sad' songs. The comment threads said, *Aww, shucks, isn't that cute. She'll be a musician! Wow, what a boyfriend he'll make.* And, usually further down, *It can't have happened without another trigger.*

But I couldn't accept that prior to his Casio meltdown, my son had been sad, had heard Greensleeves, and then associated the song with his emotion. It hadn't happened at home – and childcare, relatives or babysitters would have told us if the tragedy had occurred on their watch.

When he bawled for a third time, we put the keyboard away. Which I felt minor key about. He loved tapping it and humming along, but it wasn't worth the tragedy because it would take too long to settle him.

The Victorian music therapy community agreed our son's experience was rare. But the then sixteen-year-old daughter of Grace Thompson, Lecturer in Music Therapy at Melbourne University, had also had a meltdown as a toddler during music lessons.

'There was a piece called The Sad Donkey, and every time she heard [it] she would start to cry... I had to ask the teacher if we could skip that song...'

Thompson said her daughter was now 'perfectly "normal" in all respects' – but remained highly sensitive. It's this sensitivity that interests Nikki Rickard, Associate Professor in the School of Psychology & Psychiatry at Monash University. She suggested our son could have a case of 'extreme empathy', which sometimes means people actually feel others' physical pain, but can also see them express this emotionally.

'Empathy, and also emotional contagion, catching emotions from others, have been proposed as main reasons music can be such a powerful means of inducing emotions in us... People with more empathy will obviously feel this more strongly.'

Katrina McFerrin, Director of the National Music Therapy Research Unit, agreed that our boy's response could be an indicator of deep sensitivity.

'[It] may be attached to either a very fine sense of creativity, or a vulnerability for mental health problems, or possibly both', she said, adding that her thoughts were purely anecdotal. Another music therapist, who wished to remain anonymous, said our son's experience pointed to the possibility of him having an 'extraordinary mind', but also to being potentially high on the Asperger's spectrum.

Extraordinary mind sounds fun, Asperger's, not so much. In *Musicophilia: Tales of Music and the Brain*, Oliver Sacks told the story of American composer, Tobias Picker. His extraordinary mind allowed him to recognise and tap out tunes on a piano at our son's age, and by seven he could play complex pieces after one listen. But he constantly found himself 'overwhelmed by musical emotion'. Picker felt cursed, but still became a musician.

His story led Sacks to believe in a 'musical brain' – and new technology has shown the physiological changes that musical training brings to musicians' grey matter. It enlarges areas associated with musical ability, particularly the joining of the hemispheres.

Sacks wrote that potentially everyone had innate musicality. He cited the case of the 'Suzuki Method' used to train kids to play violin by ear and imitation only. 'Virtually all hearing children responded to such training', he wrote, adding that there may even be innate musicality in deaf kids.

This all led Sacks to consider the role of 'procedural' and 'episodic' memory in how we experience music. The former memory is held in many neural systems, which ensures it sticks. Episodic memory, the one music theorists say operates to create mood when we hear music, is built on perceptions of highly individualised experiences. Importantly, some procedural memories may be present before birth. For example, motor skill development, which begins in the womb.

Our son's response to music could be evidence for what science is demonstrating about how emotions function in the brain.

'One intriguing possibility is that his mirror neuron system is being activated', Nikki Rickard said, adding that mirror neurons have been recorded in observers of goal-directed actions, for example, a monkey feeding itself. 'Many have proposed that emotional empathy might also act in this way... an observer of emotions in another, or in music, could actually feel the emotion being expressed by the other.'

There's no definitive answer yet for the cause of our son's Greensleeves moment. Experts can only speculate. So, rather than panicking about Asperger's or depression, I'm speculating he'll play guitar better than me. Definitely piano.

When he was nearly four and, because whenever he saw our old piano's ivories he banged away on them, we brought out the Casio again. Thankfully, he was more interested in the keys – and the choo-choo train sound effect – than the recorded songs. And the only time he cried was when his big brother told him to turn it down because he was doing his homework.

12

Dad's Kitchen Rules

FIVE WEEKS INTO a six-month study exchange in Europe, coronavirus sent my twenty-year-old son back to Melbourne. He moved into his first share house, with three friends. Because restrictions meant I couldn't go inside, we went for a social distance walk to catch up.

'What do you think of my haircut?', he asked, taking off his beanie to reveal a shaved head. With his beard and height, I told him he looked like Melbourne AFL ruckman, Max Gawn.

'He looks like Max *Gaunt*', my wife said when she saw the photo of her step-son. 'He'll get the virus, he's looking so skinny. What's he eating?'

I'd walked to the supermarket with him that day and he'd bought jar sauces. Despite what anti-jar sauce YouTube campaigner 'Nats What I Reckon' was expletively telling everyone.

'He's got to learn to cook properly!' my wife implored me. Like I could just wave a wand or shoot a YouTube clip.

I messaged my son, told him of my wife's radical idea of him learning to cook with fresh ingredients, but he wasn't interested. Until I told him it would be cheaper than buying jarred stuff. I said I'd teach him, then remembered I couldn't go in his house.

I taught him over Messenger video calls. First, spaghetti Bolognese, the fast-food you make at home. He needed to feed himself and three male housemates, who were just as tall and Max Gaunt as him. There were several beards. I told him to double the recipe – two kilos of beef, one-hundred tomatoes, maybe an ox. The lesson started and he had ear buds in, but no ingredients out, not even a pot. Blokes wandered in and out of the kitchen, fascinated.

'Let's start with the garlic and onion', I suggested and, half an hour later, he finished chopping them. Thirty minutes that sounded like a road crew working, with a Bluetooth speaker pumping dance music and blokes off-camera laughing and horse playing like actual horses.

Another forty-five minutes later, we both tossed mince in our pots with carrots, zucchini, basil, tomatoes and tomato paste. Then, two hours later, a photo from my son popped onto my Messenger feed: his three, twenty-year-old mates sitting around a table eating the Bolognese my son had cooked. Every horse happy with a smile on his face and the caption 'Loving the pasta!'

His confidence was high. I put him through the same routine for butter chicken. Several photos were exchanged while he was at the supermarket trying to figure out if he was buying the right spices. He was worried, too, that it was getting expensive. I reminded him that part of the cooking lesson deal was that I'd pay him back for his ingredients. He messaged back 'forgot' and reached for the top shelves.

Wok measurements were sent and confirmed via Messenger and, once he was happy his had the right dimensions, he got butter chicken plated up to the same grins from his horse mates.

Then, due to a combination of revised restrictions, someone coming back to live at his house and someone else needing a room in a house in another state (or something), he moved back to his Mum's for a while.

'Do you still want to learn to cook?' I messaged him and he said he did. I'd thought for sure his mum would take over. But, because restrictions then allowed it, she took off to her beach house with her husband to work, so my son ended up cooking for himself and his older sister. To her amazement, he nailed a beef broccoli stir fry.

Then came his biggest test: Dad's Chicken Dish.

I was excited. It was a recipe I'd mastered from my signed copy of Stefano de Pieri's *Modern Italian Food*, now a family institution. I was grateful that, even during coronavirus separation, my son and I were set to have a moment of intimacy.

But I could have told the kid to get his chicken chopped at the butchers.

'This is it, I'm not doing any more cooking,' he told me on screen, his sister laughing in the background. His stare made her decide to go for her daily walk.

'Have you got kitchen scissors?' I asked him.

'This knife's all I've got', he said through gritted teeth. I called my wife to the screen.

'He's struggling with the bird', I said, stating the clucking obvious.

'Keep going', she encouraged him. 'Yep, it's hard... No scissors?... Yeah, your Dad should have told you to get it done at the butchers...'

Somewhere in the clatter of knives, expletives, chicken dangling, carrots and garlic chopped and olives de-pipped, I forgot to tell him to chop up the potatoes.

'*Oh*, I'm never cooking again...'

Later, with his sister, he ate his first Dad's Chicken Dish not in Dad's house. A success – the picture and caption said so.

'Very yummy! Sorry for getting so stressed about it.'

He moved to another share house where he had to cook once a week. He served his crew butter chicken first time round. It would likely be a while before Dad's Chicken Dish came out, but at least Dad was in his cooking somewhere.

13

Memories, Like Some Corners of our Lives

THE ELDERLY WOMAN THINKS I'm her late husband. It's 1990, she's in the nursing home's dementia ward, and I'm her twenty-one-year-old attendant carer. I'm trying to shower her in her purpose-built plastic chair, but she's raising herself from it, whacking my arms and trying to hit me in the face. She's yelling at me, the husband she believes I am, for being a bastard. After a while, she settles and allows the showerhead's warm spray to sooth her.

◇ ◇ ◇

On her deathbed, Shirley, my eighty-five-year-old grandmother, could smell the nectarines that used to grow on her family's Wimmera property when she was a young woman. According to my mother, Shirley smelt them, then tasted them. Then she was gone.

◇ ◇ ◇

It's 2008, I'm divorced and nearly forty, living alone next to an elderly man whom I presume to be a widower. One afternoon, Harry's on the front nature strip in his dressing gown, telling me he's lived in the area for fifty years. 'I was a ten-pound pom', he says, adding that no one he knows lives nearby anymore. 'They've all gone', he grumbles. I ask him if he was ever married and he says, no, he never saw the need for all that. The next day he tells me the same story, along with how hard it is for him to breathe at night. I wonder if he has any social connections so I ask if he goes to church. He flares up for a moment and tells me they're all a bunch of hypocrites. Then it's time to let me know again that there's no one around for him from the old days. When he dies six months later, government officials place his furniture on the lawn and ask me if I want any of it. I can't bring myself to inspect the items.

◊ ◊ ◊

I'm in Uncle Reg Blow's hospital room. The bushy grey-haired Aboriginal elder is under the bedcovers, hoping to recover from leukaemia. My five-year-old son is with me, eyeing off the didgeridoo leaning in the corner of the room. Uncle Reg has many plans for when he gets out of hospital. He's going to continue with the men's 'circle work' over which he's been presiding. I've witnessed these sessions, seen the big man's power to influence drug-affected and disorientated younger Aboriginal men. He tells me to come up close to his pillow so he can whisper what the secret is, what we need to do if we're going to see any change in the world: 'Unconditional love, Paul. That's what we're gunna need'. On his funeral order of service, a photocopied sheet, there's a headshot of him in his boxing days, wearing a woven cap. I remember then his other sage advice: 'Paul, life's like boxing: you gotta give more than you take'.

◊ ◊ ◊

Memories, Like Some Corners of our Lives

My daughter turns twenty-one and remembers being two years old and me telling her to come outside one night. I held her in my arms in the backyard and pointed at an impossibly large and chalk-white moon. And she remembers being twelve and playing volleyball in the backyard with me. I turned around, bent and picked up the ball, tried to throw it to her between my legs. I failed and the ball slammed into my bum. She laughed so much we couldn't continue the game. And, for years after, all she could say was, 'Remember the time you grabbed the ball...' and her voice would collapse into laughter.

◇ ◇ ◇

I remember, too often, the day my ex-wife and I had to explain to her and her younger brother that we'd no longer all be living in the same house. The memory still makes me catch my breath.

◇ ◇ ◇

The literary type in me knows I'm putting all these memories together as vignettes to imitate the way in which memories come at us every day: sometimes triggered by a conversation at work, a smell or a song. Could we survive them, could we even function, if they came to us any other way? If they came as full stories, novels or films, could we stand up to their power?

◇ ◇ ◇

My ex-wife texts me, tells me she's listening to the '90s band My Friend the Chocolate Cake, remembering good times we had together. For three years after we divorced, we fought over who should have the kids and how often. I was so bitter, I couldn't even see why the kids were gravitating to the Bible's story of King Solomon deciding he'd have to cut a child in half if the two desperate parents couldn't decide to whom the child belonged. My former wife's text message makes me shake with grief and love and loss and forgiveness.

◊ ◊ ◊

It's my impression that my father grew up in a house with limited love. His father rarely spoke, kept whatever feelings he had to himself. His mother, for unexplained reasons, didn't want my father. Yet she had two more children after him. She died in her fifties and I remember, as a seven-year-old, pretending to be sad and crying in mum's lap. She laughed, 'I didn't know you cared about her!' Everyone was crying, it seemed the thing to do. I didn't see my father cry; he comforted my crying mother, whom, I presume, was doing the grieving for him. He had a right to shed some tears, at least that day, for his lack of love.

He hasn't found it easy to be warm or affectionate to his sons, but he's never had an unkind word to say about anyone, has always stood up for women's equality, even at risk to his personal safety, and he's treated all age groups and races the same. This from a man who went to Sunday school as a boy in the 1950s and was whacked on the hands with a ruler, multiple times, for gazing out the window at cows in a paddock. He told me once that fishing was his religion. Then, in his sixties, after seeing a musician whose name I can't remember, he played me one of the musician's songs. The thrust of the lyric, that my father nodded along to, was that Jesus was his friend and always would be. My father doesn't have dementia, knows very well I'm his son, but when I reminded him of that day and the song, he smiled and said he couldn't remember what I was talking about.

Memories, Like Some Corners of our Lives

◇ ◇ ◇

I used to think everyone remembered faces. I can't remember names so I'd tell people, as a joke, 'Hey, at least I always remember a face'. Recently, I found I could be considered a braggart: University of Greenwich researchers in 2015 estimated that one per cent of the population are 'super recognisers', able to commit to memory even faces they see just once. Perhaps that's why, even though I'm keen on the idea of having my name written in the Bible's 'Book of Life', I'm just as enamoured as W. B. Yeats was by the face I had before the world was made. But perhaps the two ideas are the same. Maybe, in the eternal scheme, what's in a name – mine, my father's, my ex-wife's, my kids' and elderly women with dementia – will be what's written on a face.

14

UFC (Ultimate Fathering Confusion)

THE CALL FROM my then seventeen-year-old son came at the time parents dread: after eleven on a Saturday night. He wasn't a frequent visitor to my house so he must have been in deep trouble he didn't want to tell his mum about.

He'd probably been in an accident.

He or one of his unlicensed friends had stacked a car and they needed an adult who wasn't going to freak.

He knew I wouldn't freak because I hadn't when he'd had a party at my house and semi-trashed it.

'How are you, Dad?'

'I'm good, son. How are you?'

'I'm good too.'

'What's news?'

'You know how I said I'd be going to the UFC tomorrow night?'

Ultimate Fighting Championship: don't tell me he's been in a punch up? He knows less about fighting than cleaning semi-trashed houses.

UFC (Ultimate Fathering Confusion)

'Yes, I remember you were going.'

'Yeah, well, I've got a spare ticket. Do you have plans?'

No, I didn't. And it was a fact I relished.

'No, son. No plans.'

'Well, do you want to come? I'm still asking a few people...'

Chances to see him were rare so I was honoured to be a back-up plan on his social calendar. But a few hours at the UFC? I like boxing, but I had major concerns about UFC. I was worried about him going, but he told me to relax. Apparently several thousand testosterone-, steroid- and alcohol-fuelled hyper-masculine men in a large hall watching hulks tear strips off each other should make me chill.

My tall, thin son's head would be squashed cartoon-like into his Ralph Lauren polo shirt.

'I don't know if I can make it', I told him. 'What time's it start?'

'Ten thirty.'

'Sheesh, that's late.'

'In the morning...'

'Sheesh, that's early!'

What was there to fight about at ten thirty in the morning? Who put sugar in your coffee?

'Can I let you know in the morning, son? If you find someone tonight, that's fine, no stress.'

In the morning I decided if he hadn't found someone, I'd go.

'You still have the ticket?' I texted.

'Yes. U want to come?'

Want? No.

'I'll come.'

◊ ◊ ◊

At Rod Laver Arena the curly moustached security guard waved his wand over me and laughed.

'At least you'll still see the main event', he said and ushered me through. It was midday. How much could I have missed?

Inside, there was a queue for the mens toilets longer than any I'd seen for the womens, anywhere. And it wasn't as if there weren't women here, mainly dressed in tight black jeans and tighter t-shirts. Everlast and Lonsdale. The line for the mens – populated by blokes whose average bicep circumference matched my leg's – was surely the result of beer and steroids.

Where was my son?

I texted him that I'd arrived and I checked my ticket for where I had to go. A swarm of late teen and early twenties blokes in black UFC caps and t-shirts blocked my path. A few years ago, they were probably screaming at the World Wrestling Entertainment grudge matches and wearing that paraphernalia. But now they'd traded the pantomime for the real deal.

Like my son had.

The auditorium was murmuring as if it was the hour before a big concert. House lights were up, a huge crowd. I showed my e-ticket to the smiling and pleasant middle-aged female usher and got my bearings. I was on the third level.

UFC (Ultimate Fathering Confusion)

Way below, where a tennis court or U2's mid-gig busking stage should have been, sat a purpose-built, see-through cage surrounding a white canvas octagon. Inside, trainers attended the combatants, who were sitting on austere chairs at either end. It was mid-fight and there were no advertisements blaring.

People in black, sitting in chairs, dotted the cage's perimeter. I took them to be judges. Set back another two metres were the first rows of seats, the ringside tickets that cost about a grand. My ticket had cost eighty dollars. The cheap seats. I climbed the stairs to them, and every row had more beefcakes than a McDonald's delivery truck. My son wasn't in his seat, nor were his mates.

His text came in: *Just in the bathroom. Up in a sec.*

They're all in the bathroom?

A muted roar from the crowd and the large screen said we were ready to go in the final five-minute round of the scheduled three between South Dakota's Ben Nguyen and Geane Herrera from Florida.

They were flyweights.

They bounced around and bopped each other.

They kicked and punched and wrestled and scrapped and the crowd offered only muted encouragement. The round ended, the result went to Nguyen, and the fighters embraced. Then the screen went into hyper-promotion mode. For gaming, upcoming UFC fights on pay-per-view and, finally, the next bout. A decent roar went up. It would be Richard Walsh from Australia up against Canada's Jonathan Meunier in the welterweight division. I watched my son carry his backpack and climb the stairs to our seats. Alone.

'Where are your mates?' I asked as he downed the pack.

'I told you Tim couldn't use his ticket.'

'I thought you had other mates with you?'

'They're in other seats.'

'So, it's just you?'

'Yup.'

So, if I wasn't here, he'd be alone? I am a bad parent. And what of his mother? Did she know he was going to this bash fest by himself?

'Who won that last bout?' my son asked.

'Nguyen', I told him, but it seemed neither to faze nor interest him. He was focused on the build-up to the Walsh/Meunier fight. Inaudible interviews on the big screen: bald-headed Walsh, a fitter version of the meat-axe you avoid in the tradesman's aisle at Bunnings, and Meunier, a lump with the narrow eyes and square jaw of a Hollywood villain. Entourages led the real-life fighters to the side of the ring where they were inspected – for weapons? – and then ushered into the octagon. A hefty roar went up when the Australian was announced and then it was down to business.

All action, UFC business.

Walsh chased Meunier, the bookies' favourite, and I hassled my son for the rules.

'You can kick anywhere but the nuts.'

Meunier was getting on top in this first round, heavy kicks to the Australian's front leg.

'You can't poke in the eye, or twist hands or toes. And you can't head-butt.'

UFC (Ultimate Fathering Confusion)

The round finished and the older father-son pair in front of us in work wear said it went to Meunier. In the second round, the pair were on the ground for too long, not smashing each other enough, so the referee got them back to their feet. But the next two rounds and the fight went to Meunier – his kicking was accurate and hardy and Walsh couldn't, apparently, get inside and hit the Canadian with his favoured right hand.

My son finished his assessment, and ate his packed lunch. There was blood in the ring and cleaners mopped up.

The next bout saw a fighter pinned to the canvas having his head used as a totem tennis ball. The referee took a long time stopping the bout. When he did, medicos surrounded the flattened fighter. The slo-mo replay came on screen.

'Why did the ref take so long?' I asked.

'He probably thought the guy was trying some leg move', my son offered.

Another replay. It was clear to both of us the pancaked fighter wasn't doing anything with his leg but twitching it in distress.

'The ref got it wrong', my son said simply.

'Why do you like this?'

He shrugged.

'You never know what's going to happen until the end. Fighters can be downed heaps and still get up and win.'

'Almost knocked out?'

'Yep.'

And he liked the skills.

During one bout, a woman's voice screamed from in front of us that the Aussie should take care of his opponent by ripping his f*%ing neck off. Her comment was greeted by a male voice, 'Go back to Frankston!' which brought a ripple of laughter. Then there was the regular 'hit him in the penis' call. Good for a laugh, it seemed, especially with effeminate vocal intonation.

There was one women's fight on the card: Seohee Ham from Busan against Danielle Taylor from the USA. My son said he wasn't looking forward to it.

'I don't like to see women fighting', he said.

'Isn't that sexist?'

He wasn't sure. He just didn't like it.

The women looked fit and fierce. They hopped about, but no haymakers landed in the three rounds. Not entertaining enough, it seemed. They were asked a few times to hit each other in the penis. There was booing. Then numerous calls, fake shouts of excitement: woo, woo, woo when nothing was happening. That got lots of laughs. The bout was tame, perhaps to my son's taste. But it was the only tame fight. The octagon had become slippery with blood and I saw punches and kicks thrown and land that would maim or kill civilians.

Many hours after the security guard had mocked my late entry, the combatants in the main event took to the octagon: Australia's Robert Whittaker versus Derek Brunson from the United States in the middleweight division. Whittaker, then ranked seventh in the world, looked like a gym-fresh bodyguard for a Narco cartel leader. Eighth-ranked Brunson came across as a rap artist who could walk his talk without weapons.

UFC (Ultimate Fathering Confusion)

We were scheduled for five, five-minute rounds and away we went and Brunson was fighting like he wanted it over in five seconds. He chased Whittaker across the octagon with a cartoon whirlwind of punches and kicks and Whittaker could only defend, dodge and evade, which he did with some success. The formerly squealing crowd was reduced to *oohs* and *ahhs*, which gave some airspace for another call:

'Don't worry, Robbie. He's black. He'll burn out. They all do.'

My son shook his head. Then from behind us an Irish voice.

'Jesus f&*#*ing Christ. You think we've come a long way and then you hear a call like that.'

Up the Irish.

The fight changed speed and, whoops, Brunson was burning out. His tornado of blows was tiring him and Whittaker was bringing on thunder and lightning of his own. It hit hard and it hit long and Brunson reeled and the patriotic crowd screamed and rose to its feet. Fifty-one seconds into round one the referee declared Whittaker the winner. He hurled himself to the top of the fence, banged his chest, bellowed and the ecstatic crowd roared with him.

The fight hadn't even gone twenty percent of the distance, but the crowd was well satisfied. It was full of testosterone and alcohol. If any trouble was going to boil, it was now well-brewed.

I broke for the exit with my son as close to my side as possible. He's taller than me and his prissy khaki cap was surely a target. I puffed out my chest. I'm six-foot-one in the old scale and weigh ninety-two kilograms. I had enough boxing training to keep the Orcs of Mordor away from my son long enough for him to run as I was pummelled.

'Did you have a good day?' I asked, deepening my voice.

'Yeah, it was good. You like it?'

All around us there was whooping, discussions and analysis. Beefcakes, Orcs, Trolls and Big Blokes walked around quoting stats and replaying action verbally. And there were some small guys. And women. Smiling and laughing. No one was punching or kicking anyone. This kept up all the way to the packed tram. My son a thin, Bowie like figure in the crush. Headphones on, but, wait, one was coming out.

'You didn't say if you liked it.'

'I liked hanging out, son.'

He smiled and put the earplug back in.

15

Punt Flick

WHEN HISTORIANS GET SERIOUS and try to figure out when was the golden age of AFL/VFL advertising, they may agree it was the 1970s. In that great era of sponsors, which included Patra orange juice, Ballantyne cheese and Winfield cigarettes, surely the pick was the Hutton's Footy Frank. With zero nutritional value, but maximum kids-will-love-the-zany-smiling-hotdog value, the Hutton's Footy Frank was, quite obviously, purpose-built for football advertising.

When my youngest son was six, I found in a cupboard an old Hutton's Footy Frank-sponsored VFL promotional book. It contained puzzles, games, profiles, stories and quizzes for the footy mad kid of the seventies, i.e. me. I showed it to my son and, to my surprise, he loved it. I knew he was a footy mad kid of the tween decade, but I didn't think it would extend to WordFinder puzzles that included the names of footballers – Callery, Briedis, Barham – that he'd never heard Bruce McAvaney call.

Best of all for a Dad trying to keep his son away from the TV, computer, Mum's old smartphone and the iPad for at least an hour a day, the book's centrefold was a footy dice game. When I was a kid, I didn't have a clue how to play it. But, luckily for my son, his Dad is fully-grown and totally across the nuances of how to spin a dice and advance a five-cent coin up a cartoon drawing of a footy oval, dodging squares that say things like, 'Tackled!' and 'Spoiled!'.

The cartoon footy ground's grandstands were, no surprise, decorated with Hutton's Footy Franks. But the fence line was all white space. After we'd played it the first time, my son said he wanted to play it again, and went to his room to find the book. When he didn't come back for five minutes, I thought I'd better go and help. But he was busy with a black texta drawing onto the cartoon footy ground the fifty-metre arcs missing from 1970s' ovals. He was also, to my joy at his spelling ability – and horror at his skills in soaking up contemporary advertising – writing a sponsor's name multiple times on the fence: Centrebet. Centrebet. Centrebet.

The parenting gurus say if we want behaviour in our children that we don't like to go away we should ignore it. So I ignored his addition of the twenty-first century sponsor. I congratulated him instead on the introduction of the fifty-metre arcs. And got on with the game. He didn't mention the sponsors during the first quarter. Then, 'Do you like my Centrebets?'

No, son, I don't like your Centrebets. I like your writing and your creativity, but I don't like that you, who watches football fanatically, have been indoctrinated into the cult of sport gambling. In fact, it makes me want to ban you from watching football. But that would enrage you and I value my sanity. And, what's more, I like footy too. To ban you would be to ban myself.

'Umm, yeah, they're good, but we don't like gambling on the footy, do we?'

He knows that's what Centrebet is about. He's asked me before.

'No, Dad. We don't... why?'

It's a hard one to answer. For him, Centrebet is something like a Hutton's Footy Frank. But the problem is, I wanted Hutton's Footy Franks for dinner every night when I was watching the footy in the seventies.

'I don't like it because it spoils the game.'

A useless comment. It means nothing to him. For my son, the only thing that spoils the game is the Bulldogs losing.

'It's not good because gambling might make some players cheat. They might try to lose so they win a bet and get lots of money.'

He nods. Lots of money for him was the tooth fairy's delivery of a two-dollar coin. Luckily, he lost interest in the betting saga and my enjoyment or otherwise of his Centrebet ground advertising. He just enjoyed the game, and even more so when he won it.

I was mad for Hutton's Footy Franks when I was a kid. Mum would occasionally give in and buy them. They tasted much worse than the regular hot dogs she bought from the butcher, but I felt, as Hutton's no doubt hoped, like a winner when I ate them.

Unfortunately, I'm sure that if Centrebet were to read of the effects on my son of their advertising they would feel like a big team of winners. And that their multi-million-dollar ad campaign had been no gamble at all.

16

We Have the Touch

I CAN'T WATCH TELEVISION GAME SHOWS without thinking of elderly Mrs Donchi. In the early 1990s, I worked as an attendant carer to mainly older people in Melbourne's high-rise housing commission flats. Mrs Donchi lived in one in Prahran with a panoramic city view, her flat full of purple velour furnishings and the strong smell of mothballs. With permed hair and full makeup, she tried to welcome me with a smile, despite a stroke having taken away her facial muscle control. Mrs Donchi struggled to walk, but still offered to get me a cup of tea that I'd tell her it was *my* job to make for *her*.

Once I'd tidied her flat and made sure she was taking her medications, we settled with our cups of tea in front of John Burgess's *Wheel of Fortune*. And, with our eyes always on the screen, Mrs Donchi would hold my hand throughout the show. When I left, she thanked me for coming and patted my hand gently. I'm convinced she'd have foregone my tidying of her flat, the cup of tea and her medication check if it meant we could have touched hands for longer.

A younger woman I knew around the same time struggled to be touched at all. I met her at a church that placed a huge emphasis on community; it brimmed with the desire for people to be close in everything from worship to after-service wash up. Hugs, hand-holding in the pews and plutonic massages were all part of the God is Love-in. But this woman couldn't be part of it; people would try to hug her and, forcing a smile, she'd break loose like the cartoon skunk Pepé Le Pew's reluctant lover. Abandoned by her mother and finally adopted, she'd experienced very little touch in the early months of her life. She wanted to allow herself to be touched, but the idea made her freeze.

I often thought of that woman when I saw my then eight-year-old sleeping in bed alone. Families in some cultures sleep huddled together, but independent westerners allow young ones to go touch-free at night. When he was a baby – and even later – the best way to help settle him when he was angry, sad, hyperactive or tired was to scratch his back. He'd lie quietly and purr and let you do it for as long as it took for your hand to ache.

Sexuality is one of the west's biggest obsessions, but, even though touch is central to it, we don't hear touch talked about in the same way as sexuality. We're told that people missing out on sex have got something to worry about, but those missing out on touch are often overlooked. Yet scientific research reported in *Psychology Today*, even before COVID-19's social distancing, identified the individual and social costs associated with touch deprivation. Some of these seem obvious, such as lack of emotional intimacy between people, weakened team dynamics and decreased overall wellbeing. But others were more surprising; it was found that children who received limited touch had an increased chance of being violent adults. And touch was also shown to improve our immune systems and encourage greater learning engagement. The research also spoke to a kind of Midas touch effect occurring as a result of tactility. NBA teams were studied and it was shown that those that touched more often won more matches. Perhaps the Grand Final-losing Adelaide Crows of 2017, who stood apart for the national anthem throughout that AFL final series, might have been better served flocking together.

It's hard to miss in the New Testament the amount of touching in which Jesus is said to have engaged. A prostitute rubs his feet with expensive perfume, and he washes his disciples' feet as a way of showing them how to serve the world. A woman touches him in a crowd and he says he feels power go out of him. And the woman is healed.

Though he was also said to have healed people without touching them, it seemed Jesus was showing us a powerful link between the two. Perhaps it's a link akin to the one scientists have shown exists between tactility, healthy immune systems and emotional well-being. And another reason why any social force that keeps us bodily removed from each other – whether social distancing, isolation or reliance on robotics – will have its costs.

It's said we live in a visual age. So much of our working lives and leisure is linked with our sense of sight. Working at computers, staring at phones, chilling in front of subscriber TV and, less often now, at cinemas. Hearing comes in second, as we stick our headphones in on trains, listen to Siri and Google Home's alleged help, or listen to cats mewl on ubiquitous Facebook videos. It's incredible to think that the dominant force of our age, social media, a technology that is supposed to bring us closer together, engages only two of our five senses in its attempt. No wonder its relevance is being reconsidered, even by Facebook's former vice-president of user growth, Chamath Palihapitiya, who spoke of regretting having built tools that were destroying 'the social fabric of how society works'.

Social media would never have been enough for the New Testament's St Thomas. Perhaps better described in contemporary business-speak as 'solutions-based Thomas' rather than doubting, it wasn't enough for him to see and hear the resurrected Jesus standing in a room. It's only theological speculation, but it seems it wasn't enough for Thomas to smell Jesus, either. Maligned for his doubting, Thomas was desperate to put one of his other senses into play: touch. For him – and maybe for us more than we realise – touch was integral to faith and belief. Despite all our attempts to revolutionise our lives via the technology that keeps us physically apart, there's a yearning in us as deep as our humanity for the cosmic security that comes with touch.

I'm one of a group of men who meet every fortnight to talk about life's big issues. We all have our problems, hang-ups and hopes. Some of us show up to meetings in a pretty bad way. Or, perhaps more accurately, we allow ourselves to reveal to each other that we're in a bad way. Because the meetings are a judgment-free-zone, we speak our truth, however painful. We know that, unless we ask for it, we're not going to receive the problem-solving advice men are known to offer each other in lieu of emotional intimacy. But men often can't help that behaviour because practical advice and *boys don't cry* were the only guidance on male intimacy we'd received from our fathers or other male role models.

Up until I turned twenty-five, my father had hugged me once in my life, tearfully after I married my first wife. But me and the old man have, thankfully, improved the statistics since.

Matters of Life and Faith

After meetings, our group of men try to embrace rather than shake hands. We don't have to, but the offer is there. And, when we feel really advanced, we allow the embrace to last longer than a couple of seconds, while avoiding nervous back-slapping. It's not a scientific result, by any means, but I know I come home happier if I hug each of the men before we leave.

17

When the Neighbourhood's Heart Broke

MY FRIEND BRUNO had been given two months to find somewhere else to live because his landlord had decided to move into his house. After two years in Seddon, Bruno, then in his fifties and an ESL teacher at nearby Victoria University, faced an eviction familiar to so many renters.

Although he was a renter, Bruno, who has a body the size of a jockey but a heart the size of a horse, was the hub of a little community at the bottom of Charles Street. I watched his plight and yearned for a utopia in which home ownership was not only a result of wealth, hard-earned or otherwise, but also people's willingness to develop their community.

Bruno had sent me an email expressing his sadness at having to leave and I pictured the normally bubbly man quiet and hunched over boxes. I imagined him filling them with poetry books, his sons' lacrosse gear, wine bottles, a PlayStation, and the sepia photo from his mantelpiece of his elderly Mum and Dad, standing in front of the house they'd owned.

Bruno then had three teenage boys and he shared custody of them with his ex-wife. On his wage, he'd never be able to afford a house, either in the eastern suburbs where his ex-wife lived, or in Seddon. The only way he could maximise the time he had with his boys was to rent a house close to his workplace.

'It couldn't have come at a worse time', normally ebullient Bruno confessed. He'd been spending many evenings and weekends driving east, helping his mother settle into a nursing home, and helping his ailing father adjust to life without her.

In some ways, Bruno's was a typical story in our cut-throat rental market: a lower-income earner hoping to compete with professionals in the battle for high-priced properties. But his story was different because he was a community builder being expelled from his community.

Bruno knew all his neighbours, even two and three doors down, because he ate with them, played with them and drank wine on his porch with them, the spot from which he also acquainted himself with anyone he'd yet to meet. At his house warming, people who'd lived in Charles Street for years met each other for the first time and developed friendships.

His neighbours knew that, when they passed his house, they'd get words of inspiration from one of his favourite writers, an invite to one of the writers' nights he ran, or a bagful of apricots from the tree he lovingly tended in the front yard.

When my then fiancée and I moved into our rental property about a kilometre from Bruno's Charles Street mob, he extended his community's boundaries. While we received barely a nod of welcome from the homeowners in our street, Bruno sent us a Rumi poem he'd copied out by hand, entreating us to live with passion. It was signed with the words, *Welcome to the Neighbourhood!!!* A few months later, Bruno arrived at our housewarming with a bottle of wine on which he'd scrawled the same words in bold red texta.

When the Neighbourhood's Heart Broke

Bruno loves and embraces, often literally, everyone he meets and teaches: rich, poor, executive, cleaner, intellectual, dreamer, refugee, old Australian or new.

The land of the 'fair go' had gone if a man like him could even be fleetingly homeless.

'Start looking around, I suppose... There's not much I can do,' Bruno lamented when I stupidly asked him what were his plans. I silently agreed with him, then thought there must be more we could do as a society. Couldn't we stop making our houses 'investments' and make them homes again? Couldn't we consider longer, fixed-term leases?

A few weeks later, the bottom end of Charles Street lost its heart. I'm glad that, without a period of homelessness, it did quickly find a new community in which to beat, though who knows for how long this time.

18

The Cracks in Our Stars

ALONG WITH THE COVER VERSIONS of his song 'Hallelujah', the late Leonard Cohen's lyric 'there's a crack in everything/that's how the light gets in' is fast becoming his major legacy. Spiritual writers love to quote it, but its meaning deepens when heard in combination with the one preceding it: 'forget your perfect *offering*.' If we don't illuminate the stage of the spiritual journey that line represents, it's hard to accept, let alone celebrate, the cracks in everything.

Western culture demands perfection from politicians, institutions, sportspeople and even, lately, weather forecasters, while asking regular people to climb metaphorical ladders and strive for faultlessness. And that climbing and striving is honoured. It's why every year media brings us images of smiling kids who've achieved perfect VCE ATAR enter scores, while those with cracks in their scores remain unseen.

Then there are the endless rounds of performance reviews corporate staff experience. Though flawlessness isn't always mentioned, there's certainly no joy for employees if they're found to be just doing their job. No, you've got to be starring at your job. Literally, sometimes: I know of a government employee who's fed up at having to give star ratings every time she receives run-of-the-mill computer service from the IT team. 'Do you need a star rating just for doing your job?' she asks.

Especially before COVID-19, I regularly used ride share apps to get home when my wife had the car. After my ride home one night, just before I opened the door and went inside, I remembered to offer my driver a star rating. I gave him five. Because in giving him the top score for driving me two kilometres in the rain from the gym, I also sought a perfect rating from him for shutting up and being a good customer.

Inside, I turned on Netflix to watch the five-star series *Black Mirror*. And, spookily, the episode I watched imagined a near future when the star rating system had become the *only* way we conducted business, shopping and personal transactions. Your rating was your life. Those with low ratings were tantamount to untouchables, but as your overall rating drew nearer to perfection, the more blessed your life became. All the cracks in your personality and attitudes had to be hidden or the consequences were dire.

This isn't science fiction. China's facial recognition systems and artificial intelligence are being added to what's dubbed the 'Police Cloud', an interlocking citizen database that includes medical records, online purchases, travel bookings and social media comments. The end product is a single 'social credit' score for each citizen based on whether the government and fellow citizens consider them trustworthy.

Forget your perfect offering, but many of us apply a star-rating perfectionism to our spiritual lives. Especially when young, we're off trying to climb celestial ladders to a blazing sun of righteousness. When we find that after so many years we're still doing, as St Paul wrote, the very things we don't want to, we may decide the spiritual life is bunkum. Then, we don't just forget our perfect offerings, we forget any offering at all.

Yet, under the mores of a perfectionist culture, where winners are heroes and losers forgotten, the spiritual life *is* bunkum. It simply doesn't work like a self-help manual. Real spiritual development, I prefer that term to 'growth', doesn't come easy and, even when it does come, it's of no help if we want to reach our culture's heights of glory. Because the foundation of the spiritual life means at core admitting we've got cracks, we suffer, and that we'll never have a perfect offering to give to God or anyone else.

The spiritual life teaches us a different kind of success to the one our culture craves. And it's a success that's impossible without the deepest failure of everything we use in an effort to pretend we can survive in this wild universe without the spirit that brought it into being, and who even whirls in galaxies and is the humming for love in our hearts.

Fr Richard Rohr wrote that the only paths to real spiritual transformation are great love or great suffering. For many of us it's the latter. And that's a huge crack we want to avoid at all costs. I find it remarkable Christianity is linked with moral perfectionism when its founder is reported as telling stories like the one he did in the Gospel of Luke, that I'll give a quick update.

A student from Bible college comes to church and offers a prayer of thanks: 'Phew, thanks God that I'm not like the bad eggs I read about online, carjacking and robbing, and thanks that I'm not like that bad egg over there in the corner now, praying in his gang hoodie top. I fast and I tithe.'

In the corner, the bloke in his gang hoodie prays simply, 'God, have some pity on me, I'm a bad egg.'

In the episode of *Black Mirror*, the sanest person in that near future is a truck-driving, middle-aged 'white trash' woman. She's committed to having a bad egg's humility before God and humanity, which leads to her star rating dropping towards zero. Not dissimilar to the desert fathers and mothers, the truck driver disappears into a wilderness free of star ratings and her culture's search for perfection. She has nothing, but possesses everything. Her way of life rubs off on the main female character's approach and she too, with devastating clarity, lets go of the star rating system's vacuity and the people and way of life it built.

In the last scene, our young hero finds herself, not unlike St Paul, tucked away in prison for preaching her newfound ability to let go of her perfect offering. She and another prisoner begin shouting at each other the imperfections they can see in each other. And the process leads them to unutterable joy. Their perfect offerings gone, they see all their cracks and the light gets in.

19

The Tale Food Tells

MY WIFE AND I had been thinking for months about having our neighbour over for dinner. She was a widow who lived alone, and we thought she might enjoy hanging out with us and our raucous toddler. But our then nineteen-month-old's demands, my visiting children's ever-changing needs, and a complicated work schedule put us off. Inviting her over seemed all too hard.

But we inadvertently solved the problem when we visited a local Farmer's Market, headed to another friend's for dinner, and picked some food from our garden. These unrelated events suddenly made asking our neighbour over for dinner the most natural thing in the world.

We hadn't been to a Farmer's Market in the west, but my wife was fed up with dragging our toddler through the supermarket. We headed to Spotswood Primary School one Saturday morning and, from where we'd parked, the backs of canvas tents looked uninviting. We considered heading home, but persisted and hauled the stroller and our squawking toddler from the car.

We were glad we did. Instead of narrow supermarket aisles, there was a large grass pathway between organic fresh vegetables, fruit, meat, eggs... We spent a little more than usual, but the fresh air, conversations with growers and locals –

and the room for our miraculously happy toddler to free range – more than compensated.

The food in the bottom of our stroller had a story. We had eggs from a pictured rural run; garlic, capsicum and carrots from a farm near Bairnsdale, my mother-in-law's hometown; a box of peaches straight from a tree; and free-range saltbush lamb from the Otways, on special at $15 for a decent-sized roast. We'd planned to cook it that night, but then friends invited us for dinner.

They cooked us up a pungent meal of pesto, full of garlic, with a garden salad. From their garden. They had a bigger patch than ours so their odd-shaped cucumbers had room to grow. And they tasted cool and fresh. When we left that night, they gave us some, along with a batch of lemons from their tree.

The following Sunday afternoon, my wife was on a food high. Her normally relaxed manner was frantic, her eyes narrowing to pinpricks. When she's 'using', I just let her trip out around the kitchen and garden. That day it was picking the green capsicums she'd expertly grown in a small pot, and lopping off some of her Roma tomatoes. Then she fossicked for parsley, rosemary and oregano in the tiny herb garden she'd manufactured beneath the clothesline, jammed between the house and fence.

She got the lamb roast out, started squeezing lemons into it, stuffing and topping it with herbs and garlic. The capsicum was put to the knife, along with cucumber, carrots and tomatoes, and then oregano joined some olive oil and lemon juice in a dressing.

'Paul,' she called, even though I was in the room.

'Yes, chef', I replied, thinking I'd soon have a kitchen-hand's task. But she just told me to invite our neighbour over for dinner.

Two hours later, she was at the table, nodding and smiling (politely?) as we told her the story behind every item of food she ate. The Spotswood Primary School's Farmer's Market, that's where we got the lamb you're eating, from the Otways, it's delicious, yeah. And the lemons and cucumber from our friends; they're a lovely couple, got a baby like us. The tomato, herbs, capsicum; my wife's an amazing gardener, so little space, but such a big yield. And the peaches, tell me they're not the best you've eaten ... Oh, and the garlic: grown near Bairnsdale. We have family there. Where's your family from?

The food was the conversation, but in unexpected ways. Every item led to a new discussion, about politics, education, healthy eating – even the local council's hated plan to chop down the trees on our nature strips. Our neighbour told her own food gardening stories and we developed a manifesto that everyone in Melbourne must cook a meal at least once a week with ingredients only from Farmer's Markets and their own gardens.

When she left, we realised why it'd been suddenly easy to ask our neighbour over. When it was our own food, we wanted to tell the stories behind it, and somehow Farmer's Market food was as much 'ours' as that from our garden and our friends. 'It seemed wrong to have that lamb in the fridge and not have her over,' my wife added. Like any good story, food with its own tale to tell has to be shared.

20

A Quartet of Hope

1

COMMUNITY SPIRIT CAN BE RARE in some parts of Melbourne. Especially before COVID-19, people raced from work to social and kids' commitments, rarely stopping to talk or find common ground. Heads bowed to phones on train commutes, stuck in gridlocked cars. Children playing on the street were a rarity, and neighbours often barely knew each other, and some didn't want to add the burden of that relationship to their lives.

Without fanfare, 'Marco', a crossing guard at a local school, worked against that spirit of disconnection. Each morning, up to a hundred students and their carers used the particular path to school his crossing inhabited. 'Hello, Julian, good morning, Samantha – how was your trip to Queensland?' If it was only one family he addressed this way, it'd be a refreshing reminder of the value of knowing each other and being known. But, amongst the bip bip of traffic lights and purring of engines, Marco had these conversations with nearly anyone from the school who passed his smiling face and Stop sign.

2

A close friend attended the funeral of his uncle 'Rob' at a bland and dusty church in a Geelong suburb. Family and friends in ill-fitting suits and t-shirts in various shades of black smoked as many cigarettes as they could before they entered the sanctuary. Looked like they expected a long ceremony. Inside, however, one of the dead man's nephews made the service entertaining with a witty speech articulating the ups and downs of his uncle's colourful life.

Rob had travelled the state for employment and had difficulty holding a job. He struggled to sustain relationships and was dedicated to the booze. Once, when riding the bus after a night out drinking, he almost missed his stop and leapt from the moving vehicle, carrying a full six-pack of beer. Apart from a few scratches and fizz, Uncle Rob and his cargo were unharmed.

He dried out enough to hold regular employment and landed a job as a cleaner at the prestigious Geelong College. In his years there, Uncle Rob became a popular figure. His homespun – and hard-won – wisdom resonated with collegians, and they'd go to him for advice and guidance in tough times.

College leadership noted that, in Uncle Rob, there was another leader amongst them, even if his job title might be described as at the lower end of the hierarchy. They made the courageous and unprecedented decision one year to ask Uncle Rob, the college cleaner, to give the keynote address at the valedictorian dinner. This last shall be first arrangement continued until Uncle Rob's retirement. Year after year, he imparted his street-wise insights to successive graduates who would go on to lead businesses and organisations, surely with an understanding that not all leadership comes from the top.

3

In 2009, Jonathan Cornford decided his previous international aid work and higher education study into Christianity's response to capitalism could, with the help of his wife Kim and their children, be made into a ministry. Then based in Footscray and now in Bendigo, Jonathan began 'Manna Gum', what he described in a recent newsletter as 'truly an experiment in faith.'

More than a decade on – and, with his family, living on a wage a little over half the national average – Jonathan has published books and given talks nation-wide on how to live a life of faith in God in the context of a capitalist system. Challenging, erudite and thought-provoking, Manna Gum's tri-annual newsletter contains hard-hitting and biblically grounded treatises. His essays give insights into how people can manage their domestic economies when confronted with capitalism and consumerism's lures and traps.

In the 2015 encyclical, *Laudato Si'* – 'On Care for Our Common Home', Pope Francis wrote that '[s]ince the market tends to promote extreme consumerism in an effort to sell its products, people can easily get caught up in a whirlwind of needless buying and spending.' He said this 'compulsive consumerism' was an example of 'the techno-economic paradigm', which 'leads people to believe that they are free as long as they have the supposed freedom to consume. But those really free are the minority who wield economic and financial power.'

Mainly eschewing social and digital media, Jonathan Cornford has leant considerable theological depth to the Pope's points for many years, sending his printed message via post to seven-hundred worldwide newsletter subscribers tri-annually.

'It is a modest little publication,' Cornford writes in it, 'but feedback continues to testify that it offers something... largely missing in the Christian world: an ongoing reflection on the theological, analytical and practical challenges of living out our Christian faith and witness in the context of a crazy and destructive global economy.'

4

'Nick' is in his fifties and part of a suburban Melbourne church's congregation. Sort of. He finds it hard to sit still in church services, struggles with having so many people close to him at once, and is highly resistant to church services' propensity to have people 'talking at him'. So, instead of occupying a pew, he tends to the church garden during services, and hangs around the edges when it's time for the after-service cuppa and chat.

He drives a beaten 1990s Nissan Urvan, has moved around a lot since his marriage broke up, and he's glad he's found a rental property, even though it's on a six-lane highway. It's a house in which the landlord has said he can stay for the next three years and, for a double bonus, the already low rent will not increase – and Nick can make whatever improvements he wants to the property.

When he moved in, the house was rundown. Cracks in the ceiling, roof leaks, a barely functional kitchen, and holes in the floorboards that exposed the dirt below. A handyman, Nick was in his element. He set up a basic carpentry workshop under a tin shelter in the backyard and went to work. The house's externals are now reconditioned, Adobe style, and the kitchen is clean and neat. There are no leaks and the floorboards are fully functional.

But Nick's desire to tinker and improve didn't stop at the boundaries of his house. The council recently tore down some nature strip trees which were, apparently, causing problems for the telephone wires. That left the bus stop outside Nick's house exposed to the sun.

With Australia suffering its hottest summer on record that year – and passengers blasted by heat right outside his door – Nick got to work. Using scrap metal and material extracted from landfill, he fashioned a large umbrella underneath which the would-be bus riders could shelter. Though people can't say for sure who to thank, a glance into Nick's front yard, strewn with scrap in the process of being constructed into other helpful household and garden items – laundry baskets, shelving and steel trellises – would give them a good idea who'd cared for their sweltering bodies that summer.

21
A Christmas Carol Confession

I HAVE A NUMBER OF CONFESSIONS to make, but this one's least likely to cause panic in a general audience. Or maybe not. Anyway, here goes: from 1 December until Christmas Day every year, I pick up my acoustic guitar and sing at least three Christmas Carols per day.

I play them to visitors, my kids, my wife – I play them to myself when they've gone to bed. I play them despite the tinny versions that blurt constantly from supermarket and department store speakers. I play them despite some people's outright hatred of them, and despite their often corny lyrics (Frosty the Snowman), austere melodies (Hark the Herald Angels Sing) or bombast (O Come All Ye Faithful).

I've yet to find anyone who finds my response to the Christmas season appropriate. When I tell most people, they smile and think I'm joking. They know my music taste runs to the alternative, and that my piousness runs to the non-existent: I often get anxious just thinking about going to church, I'm not a brilliant pray-er, I tend to melancholy, and I've done things in my years of alleged faith that most proper Christians would frown upon.

A Christmas Carol Confession

I am, like my namesake St Paul, a chief sinner. Only he managed, finally, to get the job of being a decent Christian done. I often see myself as just chief in charge of sin. So maybe that's the reason why, in my house and, I'm guessing, my entire suburb, I'm chief in charge of warbling Christmas Carols for a month. By singing those sweet little songs, I'm probably trying to purge the darkness that's accumulated in me throughout the year.

It's definitely not about the baby Jesus, either. Well, maybe a bit. Some people tolerate Christmas Carols – even mine – because they mention the cute little bubba in swaddling clothes with nowhere to lie down and cry. But I'm not drawn to singing Christmas Carols because they bring out my paternalism and I fondly relive scrambling around on the nursery floor for my youngest's spat dummy. I'm not drawn to the baby Jesus, but I am drawn to the adult Jesus's vulnerability.

If you put aside all the trappings – tinsel, turkey and tolerating family – Christmas is about the God of the universe becoming a human being. A baby. Even more humble than that, a baby born in a hick town via a woman raised in a bogan province. And even humbler, she gave birth to the little guy where cows did their business.

I sing Christmas Carols for a purge, yes, but I also sing them because they're humble – and I am humbled as I sing them. There's nothing cool, funky or hip about them. Uncharacteristically, I put my Bad Seed pride and storm-cloud depression away when I sing those simple songs. I become vulnerable, openhearted... there's suddenly room for the Christmas spirit. The actual one. Even if others think I'm possessed by some hammy yuletide spirit of horror.

People can poo poo Christmas Carols all they want. I'm sure they will. I'm sure they'd poo poo them even more if they heard me singing them. But hidden in most of them is the story of a big shot (God) deciding that the best way to touch hard hearts was to get down on their level. And that keeps me strumming and hoping that one of the hard hearts the Christmas spirit breaks into each year will be mine.

22

It's an Emergency. Take a Seat.

I'M HERE BECAUSE I'VE BEEN STABBED. That's what I should have said. But, no, I choose the truthful path when the nurse behind the Emergency Department's glass security panel asks how she can help.

'I had an operation on my stomach here a few weeks ago. I'm bleeding from the wound. A little.'

'Is it in a spot where I can take a look?'

It is. Just.

'Hmm,' she says, looking at the purple blobs. 'Put one of these on it.' She hands me some hospital gauze and I rip open the pack. 'Take a seat,' she adds. 'Keep pressure on the wound. And, oh, I need to warn you: it could be a long wait.'

Before I limp to my plastic blue seat, she explains why the wait will be especially long: I've come in after eight at night. The number of doctors working behind the heavy automatic doors has, as a result, fallen from eight to three.

Great, I think. Could be a couple of hours.

I settle in to read Grahame Greene's *The Quiet American*. I've been reading a lot during my post-surgery, morphine-hazed recovery. My surgery had gone well, but then I'd got a hematoma (a localised blood clot) in the wound. It'd blown up, caused horror-movie pain, landed me back in hospital, and then back home with said morphine.

And now I'm in emergency again, with bleeding I don't understand, that my GP when I phoned her said shouldn't be happening, and I can't read properly because I need to keep one hand pressurising the wound while the other holds the book. Then there's the distraction of the TV playing US blockbuster inanity, and the strangers trickling into the emergency waiting room. Which make the Vietnam described in *The Quiet American* seem as relaxing as a spa retreat.

First comes a homeless guy in a fishing jacket who stands in front of the TV and turns it up. It was already thump-bucket loud, but now it's a Marshall stack. The guards arrive and offer him directions to the door. He takes them after a few garbled remarks about his normal routine being interrupted. I have my usual wave of hopelessness about where the hell he and others like him will sleep tonight. But the fact is, still in a bit of pain and bleeding like a squeezed cherry, I couldn't be much help to him tonight, anyway.

Then comes the drug-addled woman with brutally short black hair and tree trunk legs. She tells the nurses to get f#%#, everyone in the waiting room to get f#%#, and her ex- and whomever was associated with her ex- to get f#%#. The guards don't come. There are kids around. Families. She sits in the front row of seats and occasionally chants threats at passing nurses and patients, then at numerous unnamed enemies on the ceiling. Eventually, she gives up waiting for whatever

It's an Emergency. Take a Seat.

emergency she needs help with, goes outside, has a smoke, and disappears. And when she does, I have my usual 'why didn't I go up and say something to her, ask if she was all right' guilt trip. Cherry stains on my gut are again my excuse.

The next guest's more entertaining. She blusters in wearing a massive white skirt, her hair in ponytails and carrying an acoustic guitar strapped to her back. She loudly tells the charge nurse she's hearing voices, they aren't speaking nicely, either, and it happens from time to time. They should call her mother in Queensland.

'Anyone else that could be called?' the nurse asks, and the woman names someone who might be a housemate or a bus driver.

The minstrel guided by voices sits in the front row. She strums her guitar. She speaks loudly to the elderly couple next to her about various problems Aboriginal people face. She's as white as her skirt, but her politics are sound. She tires of them though and puts her guitar down. She stands in front of the emergency crowd and sings 'Strangers in the Night' poorly at top volume. A hipster guy with a broken hand and his girlfriend smile. The rest of us stare blankly. Our minstrel's soon ushered towards the doctors behind those heavy automatic doors.

A middle-aged woman in a rain jacket, after numerous trips to the charge nurse, finally gets her elderly mother, whose been experiencing heart trouble, through the doors. The guy with the broken hand gets through. Another elderly woman and her husband – I can't tell who's the sick one – get through. I've been up to the nurse a couple of times to get a new gauze so I decide to do it again. See if going up slices your wait time.

I've been waiting two and a half hours.

'I'm sorry,' the nurse says. 'We're really busy tonight.'

I've seen the ambulances come in. People are taken out of them and wheeled into the wards behind the nurse's station. They don't even have to go through the swinging saloon doors. I go back to my seat. I'm bleeding, in a bit of pain, unsure what's happening, starting to panic, getting pretty tired – and I've run out of money to buy chips or a packet of M&Ms. I haven't brought my credit card with me. But I'm not in half the trouble of the minstrel, homeless guy, drug-addled woman or the others I've seen enter, whose families have sweated and cried.

I can't read or watch TV so I watch a family. If they were wearing hipster clothes or something from South Yarra, I might not have noticed them. That's not entirely true – their second child is spending most of the night crying. And the dad has to keep rocking the kid or pushing her up and down in the stroller. He's lean with neck tattoos and a black Adidas sweat top. The mum's overweight, bottle blonde, wearing leopard skin pants and suffering from an unknown illness. The other child, a girl, is about eight and talks all the time about nothing in particular, when she isn't colouring in or watching the inappropriate Hollywood blockbuster. I notice them because, locked into the stereotype, I've been expecting them to soon start up a loud, expletive-driven and perhaps drug-fuelled fight. Or one parent will burst out crying and leave. Or they'll start swearing at their kids and whack them. I sit there bleeding and waiting for it. It has to happen. They've been here longer than me. But the only time they've gone to the counter is to get the baby's bottle warmed up. Neither have raised their voices at the kids. They have a lot of pressure on them; the kids are agitated and tired. But they don't get angry at each other. They just go about being a family as best they

It's an Emergency. Take a Seat.

can. But I wonder why they're all here. Only the mum's sick. Then I overhear. They were out at the time she got sick, they didn't have a car, the trains were too far to walk the kids to, and they could only afford one taxi. These are the years before rideshare, so they wait.

I'd spent the five bucks I'd brought on junk food. Maybe it could have helped them? Why hadn't I brought more money? Why can't I get the words that I want to say to these parents out of my mouth? You're doing a brilliant job! Because it's patronising, idiot, I think, so shut up.

I sit complaining about my bleeding and my little bit of pain. It'll be gone, hopefully soon, and I'll go back to my life in which I can take a taxi any time I want.

The woman in leopard skin gets to go behind the big doors and her family goes with her, to come out again about an hour later. Others enter the emergency waiting room while they're gone. They get through the doors before me. Should I go back up to the counter? I need sleep. I've been waiting five hours. I go and tell the nurse how long I've been on the plastic seat. I tell her if I'm not going to get looked at tonight I need to go home, get some sleep, and return to my spot at their deli again tomorrow morning. She manages a smile.

'I'm sorry it's been so long. I'll see what's going on.'

I'm through the doors five minutes later, on an emergency ward maxi chair being told there isn't much they can do about the bleeding. I just need to keep pressure on it and hopefully it will go away.

'Sometimes hematomas bleed. It's rare. But they do it.'

Next to me, curtains around her, the minstrel's singing. I don't know the song, but it's not a lullaby. I want out, and I want out now.

I leave with a referral to see my GP. Still in a bit of pain, limping, but thankful the night's over. I go to the free taxi phone and lift the receiver. A recorded voice says a taxi will automatically arrive. I plan to get some money or my credit card out of the house when I get home. But no taxi comes. I add a fifteen-minute wait to my five hours, but still no taxi. I walk home bleeding, feeling that, in a strange way, I have been stabbed after all.

23

Competing to be Normal

BEFORE COVID-19 SHOWED US it could slow down, if you lived in a busy city like Melbourne, you could have been forgiven for thinking life was a competition. And you were in it whether you wanted to win or not.

It starts at dawn and doesn't stop until you hit the pillow. The battle for a car parking space at the train station, the fight for somewhere to stand in your rail carriage. If you drive or ride to work, the near blood sport of being behind the wheel or on the pedals. At work, many of us compete with people we call colleagues for roles and promotions in what we're regularly told are highly competitive industries. We better keep on competing or risk sliding down social and economic ladders.

There's subtle and not so subtle pressure mass and social media puts on us to be richer, fitter, prettier, happier and smarter than everyone else. And we need to be better parents, lovers and friends than our peers. Even amateur punters sometimes face an extra burden: already in a stressful competition, they could sign up to compete against professional gamblers, just in case their competitive juices weren't flowing enough.

I have two adult children and another in primary school. Technology, hairstyles and football finalists have changed in the period between my older kids' and younger one's gigs at two different primary schools. But one thing's stayed the same: primary school emphasises collaboration and teamwork, kindness and respect towards peers and adults, and, importantly, the value of participation rather than competition. And experience tells me this set of values continues into the middle years of secondary school. Then, it all gets reversed.

Okay, maybe not the *expectation* that kids will offer each other, teachers and elders some level of kindness and respect. But from Year 10 on, they're in a battle against their peers Australia-wide. They have to compete for spots at universities that will supposedly guarantee them the opportunity to, well, continue into their adult life the competition for which late secondary school has groomed them.

Then, it's competition all the way. A materialist and consumerist culture demands it. If they're not competing in the game of life – with themselves and others – they won't feel the need to buy the latest model cars, phones, TVs and clothes. Nor will they want the best house in the best street, a suite of self-help books to assist them to compete (*Rich Dad, Poor Dad* anyone?) or holidays they can brag about. And, if they don't compete, the theory goes that the economy will collapse. The products and services our competitive businesses offer are only valuable to many of us if we think we're missing out and our peers are ahead.

None of this is surprising from an evolutionary perspective: we're part of the animal kingdom and we've had to compete for millennia to survive against dangerous beasts. But contemporary scientists are now showing the world what Catholic priest and scientist Teilhard de Chardin explained last century: it's 'love energy' not competition that makes the universe function. As David Bohm wrote in his 1995 book, *Wholeness and the Implicate Order*, quantum physics tells us the idea 'fragments are separately existent is evidently an illusion... the attempt to live according to the notion that the fragments are really separate is, in essence, what has led to... pollution, destruction of the balance of nature, over-population, world-wide economic and political disorder and the creation of an overall environment that is neither physically nor mentally healthy.'

Competition might be in our DNA, but as we evolve spiritually it seems clear that competition's an instinct we need to outgrow, for our own and the planet's sake. And, while sport's social role has differed across the centuries, perhaps its role now is to provide the best forum for the expression of our competitive instincts so that they can do the least social damage.

Many sociologists would disagree, not least of whom is Eric Anderson who in his recent book *Inclusive Masculinity: The Changing Nature of Masculinities* writes at length against the notion of sport's 'socio-positive value'. While it's hard to disagree entirely with his thesis that sport does more social damage than good, even Anderson notes it does have value when it comes to teamwork and, when men are considered, the possibility of relating emotionally in ways not permitted in other spheres. He also writes that sport is a forum for people, again historically men, to unite in 'physical joy, pain and labour'. In short, it can be a positive outlet for our competitive instincts.

Perhaps, however, that's more likely in amateur sport where the results of the competition amount to little more than bragging rights. If we look at the Australian Open tennis, the nation's biggest sporting event, we often see clearly the beasts born when our competitive DNA meets sport and 21st century consumerist-materialist culture. We've had players like Bernard Tomic and Destanee Aiava publicly admit they hate playing the sport and only do it for the money. The latter once said that when she'd made enough, she'd stop playing. She aimed to have the money to buy her own apartment and houses for her separated parents. It was unclear whether that would be enough, or whether she'd have to compete, as a tennis player and a western consumer, for more than that.

Franciscan author and spiritual teacher Fr Richard Rohr says the world order teaches us we 'win by winning', but Jesus' life teaches us we 'win by losing'. He adds that shouldn't be a hard one for Christians to figure out, given that Jesus died a criminal's death.

Anyone trying to follow Jesus', Gandhi's or St Francis's examples of downward mobility in contemporary Australia, especially its cities, will grapple with the competitive nature of our lives here. We'll feel pressure to have more of everything and to fight for more space on the road or on trains. We'll be told tortoises not only lose the race, they get stampeded and their shells sold to the highest bidder. But still, if we want to listen, there's a quiet voice in our hearts saying whomever would lose their life for the sake of love will find it.

24

Poetry with Bruce and Bunjil

FROM THE PINE BALCONY of the Lake Tyers Indigenous Training Centre, you look down a grassed slope to the water. Grey clouds mill around, but the lake above the shoreline gums still sparkles and glows. It's 'Bung Yarnda' land, home to the Lake Tyers Aboriginal Trust where two-hundred Aboriginal people live. Bung Yarnda was a mission for more than a century until it was handed back in 1970 to its original owners, the Gunai/Kurnai people, and the descendants of other Aboriginal people who'd been forcibly moved there.

Whitefellas don't get invited here often. I'm with Bruce Pascoe, Aboriginal author of *Dark Emu*, and together we're running poetry workshops. Bruce is stern-faced as he grips the timber railing with his weathered hands. It's been a tough morning as we've worked to win the participants' trust. And tried to help people, one of whom's a painter, to see how poetry could be a vehicle for stories they want to tell.

'Ah, there's Bunjil,' Bruce says, pointing at an eagle soaring above the gums. 'Good of him to be here.'

I watch the bird careen then disappear behind the gums, hoping the Aboriginal creator deity's visit will put wings on some of the participants' creativity. Later, I'm on the balcony again, this time with the painter. She's struggling to figure out how this poetry thing works. Several pelicans flap over the gums and on across the lake. 'Hey, that's *lucky*', she says, giving the birds their name from her language. 'You don't see that many together often.'

She heads back inside to grapple again with my poetry exercise and I wrestle with her lesson. Her pelicans – and Bruce's eagle – have shown me again what divides Aboriginal Australians from many of us: they are, by a Western definition, nature-mystics.

I've worked with members of an Aboriginal community before and people who've wanted to write poetry, but never both together. The Lake Tyers group took on this poetry project because they were interested, not because they were fans of T.S. Eliot or even Oodgeroo.

You want us to write this poetry stuff, you show us why we should.

I come out with a speech about poetry's similarity with painting, some other ramble about stories in snapshot and the sharp view of a moment poetry can offer. I might even have said something about how poetry can have colour and movement. I don't remember, but I felt inspired.

The painter has an *ah-ha* moment. Bruce had already given her and the other participants powerful speeches about the need for Aboriginal stories, how there are parts of their peoples' histories, Australia's history, that only they can tell. The painter's ah-ha moment becomes a poem. Her debut in verse.

'I didn't know I could do this.'

She's a single mum with two adolescent sons, the youngest of whom is watching his mum make her discovery. He looks up from the graffiti style art he's sketching. He goes back to it, with what looks to me like more purpose.

'That made sense, what you said,' his mum smiles, and she shows me her poem about the difficulty of making changes in your life when you're Aboriginal. It's fresh, the words heartfelt. Later, this painter who didn't think she could write a poem records herself reading it with her eldest son backing her on guitar.

Over three days, participants tell difficult, tragic, bright and hopeful stories in poetry. I hear about purpose-built shelters that saved kids from getting a beating from rampaging drunk whites. Poems about how participants' animal totems revealed themselves to them in the wild, and others about yearning for lost culture. Some lines imagine looking at earth from the moon, swimming with sharks, days when trees should be allowed to be pink. But always there's the revelation of how Aboriginal culture can't die, and how the Dreamtime, like the Christian view of the reign of God, is both now and forever.

The workshops finish and I'm driving the highway back to Melbourne. Some Aboriginal people have learnt, to their amazement, that they could write poetry. They had giant stories to tell that fitted neatly into just a few lines on a page. But, as usual, they've taught me more. I'm seeing rivers as living creatures, clouds and birds as messengers, and hearing the heartbeat in sunsets. The participants – and Bruce – have woken in me again a poetry that has nothing to do with pages, words, rhymes or Western understandings of meaning.

25

The Home Monastery

I'M WRITING FROM THE MIDST of Victoria's second period of lockdown during COVID-19. What we're going through has been compared to prisoners and asylum-seekers' experiences, so we've been encouraged to empathise with their plight. Whether or not we're doing that, our time shut away, especially for those who live with others, has also been compared to life as a monk or nun.

In 2013, I stayed for a few days as a guest at a traditional monastery in country Victoria. I had the deep spiritual experience I'd hoped for, but I left feeling sorry for the monks and nuns. They lived in a beautiful environment, with views of a lake and cows on rolling hillsides, but they were confined to the property. Even their bluestone-housed single rooms faced each other inside a locked courtyard.

There was some time each day when they could use the internet. They could also leave the monastery for a half-day each week, but that was the extent of their experience of the outside world. They couldn't go where they wanted, when they wanted. They were in permanent lockdown and I was sad for them, even though the spirituality one monk had developed at the monastery was instrumental in me having the deep experience I'd craved.

Like many, I've read the spiritual wisdom and ecstatic experiences of monks and nuns like St John of the Cross, Julian of Norwich, St Teresa of Avila, and the more contemporary Thomas Merton. But I realise I've ignored them when they've told me how tough the journey to Christlikeness can be.

Now, in my little COVID-19 monastery, I'm exhausted all the time from work commitments and home schooling. I'm finding it challenging to deal every day with the same loved ones in close proximity. It's becoming obvious to me why so many monks and nuns made beer, wine and other than holy spirits. But I know lockdown's better than being in ICU or spreading the virus around and contributing to the mortality rate. And I also know that lockdown's suffering is creating in me a unique opportunity to allow the spirit to work.

The gifts of the Holy Spirit quoted in Galatians 5 have always appeared to me more like holy grails. I'd look at them and think, yes, I'd love a little more love, and some extra joy would be joyous. But I read the list again recently and realised that, only due to lockdown, I'm building a just a bit more patience. That's miraculous because I'm normally the bloke tapping his foot in the supermarket queue or drumming his fingers on the steering wheel at the red light. But lockdown has given me no room, almost literally in our smallish house, for impatience with my partner and son.

Like monks and nuns, we're constantly confronted with each other's foibles. Every niggling habit – from my 11-year-old son's love affair with noise, singing to himself and humming, to my wife's joyous daily abandonment of tidiness – can have cartoon steam forming in my ears. I've seen, too, that my habits are regularly making their temperatures rise. And that's without considering the extra demands constant work from home and home-schooling have placed on our household.

But, somehow, I'm taking more deep breaths than ever. Realising that, if I lose my patience now, dropping a dish I'm putting in the machine because my son has thumped past me with his headphones on while my partner deals with a stressful work call loudly in a nearby room, what's going to stop me from losing it again and again?

What *ever* stops me from losing my patience again and again? In a way, before lockdown, before losing my patience in front of my family didn't mean having to then spend almost every minute of the day with them, *nothing* really stopped me. Patience was a quaint idea. Now, it's a necessity. Because, in our little monastery, if one of us is letting a fruit of the spirit rot, the rest of us have to smell it all day, every day.

Thomas Keating wrote that people who decide to live in a monastery to escape the world are in for a shock. Because the world's magnified within the cloister. And so also is our lockdown opportunity magnified to allow temporary suffering to prune our spirit trees and get some fresh spring fruit growing.

Still, I hope you're reading this when our patience is being tested again in, to paraphrase ecclesiological terminology, ordinary times.

26

Silence is Not Always Golden

I LIKE THE WAY in which God is said to have spoken to Elijah in the Bible's 1 Kings 19:

'Then a great and powerful wind tore the mountains apart and shattered the rocks before the Lord, but the Lord was not in the wind. After the wind there was an earthquake, but the Lord was not in the earthquake. After the earthquake came a fire, but the Lord was not in the fire. And after the fire came a gentle whisper. When Elijah heard it, he pulled his cloak over his face and went out and stood at the mouth of the cave. Then a voice said to him, 'What are you doing here, Elijah?''

I was born and raised in quiet country towns, but now live in what seems to be a constantly noisy city. It's an appealing idea that the divine's more likely to speak when the world and everything in it shuts up, especially because it adds a layer of holiness to my obsessive, decades-long search for pure silence: I might get to hear the voice of God.

As anyone who's tried it knows, finding pure silence, especially in the city, is almost impossible. Get up early and meditate and you can bet the dog next-door will start yapping, or the house being renovated two doors down will need a concrete pour. Try the same meditation in the middle of the night, in my area, and you'll experience the joys of several red-eye flights cruising just nine-hundred feet above your tiled roof.

To my great consternation, when I visited a monastery on a silence quest, a dad with two screeching toddlers occupied the guesthouse for the first few hours. It was as if the silence-dwelling divine said, 'Then a great and powerful pair of kids, the like of which he could easily listen to at home, tore the guestroom apart and shattered Paul's silence...' and ha, ha, isn't that hilarious?

My search for silence is complicated by the fact that I live with misophonia, a disorder thought to be a combination of genetics and social conditioning. It means certain sounds cause me discomfort similar to what most people feel when they hear fingernails scraped across a blackboard. I say similar, but not quite; like most with misophonia, I feel a combination of extreme anxiety and rage when I hear my trigger sounds, which makes me want to destroy the cause of the sound or hide from the world with my ears plugged full of foam.

My trigger sounds are thumping hi-fis, buzz-saws, dogs barking, planes and helicopters. Only the helicopters are relatively rare in my area. The prevalence of the other sounds means that, due to the rage and anxiety I've experienced over the past four years, I've found it hard to function normally, let alone find any silence or a divine voice emanating from it. And, if I'm not actually hearing my trigger sounds, I'm hypervigilant as I anxiously await their arrival.

An audiologist and misophonia specialist gave me an approach to the condition that apparently one woman tried and her misophonia was cured in two years. My experience of the condition has been so debilitating that when my specialist said *two years*, it felt to me like she was saying two minutes. *Two years*? Wow, fabulous! I leapt at even the remote possibility I could be healed of this aural torment.

All I have to do is, ironically, avoid silence.

My trigger sounds announce themselves in my normal range of hearing like explosions and, as a result, I cower in anxiety then bubble with anger. My treatment aims to take what I hear as strong winds, earthquakes and firestorms and turn them back into normal daily sounds. This is done by ensuring I have another low-level sound – white noise – constantly in my ears. I choose eternal loops of waves crashing or birds twittering near a stream. When my trigger sounds come, I refocus my hearing on the white noise and add a bit of cognitive therapy, speaking the trigger sound's name aloud and reminding myself that it's just a noise, noises are normal and they're nothing to fear.

I could be looking at two years with earbuds in. But it's worth a try and, thankfully, I only have to do it while I'm at home; I'm one of the lucky misophoniacs who doesn't experience the problem when out.

My son asked me why I have earbuds in constantly and I told him that, the same way bodies need retraining after they're injured, so too do brains.

This therapy, of course, puts an end to my search for silence. To continue it would, in fact, negatively impact my chances of being free from debilitating anxiety and steaming rage. So I've had to rethink my attitude to and definition of silence.

I had for many years pursued aural silence as a holy grail for personal peace, but I needed to find silence within. Despite working at meditation and contemplation for long stretches, I hadn't computed that inner silence was their goal. I would hear my internal chatter, return to my meditative mantra or contemplative object, and then for a few moments the silence within would emerge. But, as well as soon getting entangled again in my internal chatter, I would also become agitated if I heard any sound, not just my triggers.

I thought the voice and presence of the divine could only truly be found in external silence. My interpretation of the 1 Kings 19 verse was complicit in this, the idea that if I could escape all the noise, naturally occurring or human-made, I'd find a peace that passed all understanding. Now I know that if a divine whisper is going to speak to me, it will to come out of the silence I allow to emerge within myself. A deep, dark, wonderful silence that, unbeknown to me for decades, I carry around with me all the time. I can try to allow myself to enter it, whether my trigger sounds are coming, my white noise is flowing or the noisy city is doing what it does best.

It makes me want to re-write 1 Kings 19:

'Then a great and powerful dog barked madly in a backyard and shattered the silence I was seeking, but the Lord seemed to say don't worry about the dog. After the dog there were jets, but the Lord seemed to impress upon me to forget about the jets. After they flew past there came a hi-fi thumping, but the Lord said, really, you can't escape it. And after the hi-fi came a gentle whisper. When I heard it, I pulled out my earbuds and went and stood in the front yard. Then a voice said to me, 'Forget about seeking silence and let the silence within you be my presence."

27
Everything Under the Sun

I'M SURE I'M NOT ALONE in the universe in that, as a child, I wrote out in detail my place in the universe. Pre-empting my later love of words, my seven-year-old self scrawled this at the bottom of the family Scrabble board:

> Paul Mitchell / 4 Scott Court, Korumburra / Victoria / Australia / World / Solar System / Galaxy / Universe.

Even before Korumburra, my street and town had changed five times because of my dad's work with a bank. And, after Korumburra, it would change another thirteen times before I'd land in my current home.

Current *house*. The adage that a house doesn't make a home has always sat easily with me. I moved around so much that becoming attached to a house was stupid, and to lock the esoteric notion of 'home' into bricks, mortar, weatherboards and nature strips even more so.

Wanting to feel at home is as natural as breathing and it's remained something for which I've yearned. But my scrawl at the bottom of the Scrabble board didn't help bring me any closer to it. Registering my galactic address just showed me I was too small and the universe too big.

I didn't have a religious upbringing and I was petrified of death. In bed at night, I'd stare into the ceiling's blackness and know I was a tiny blip whose light would snuff out and everything I did, said or hoped for would be useless. And my flesh crawled with terror.

Mum would tell me not to worry, that death was for old people. She'd try to calm me by telling me to think about happy things. One of her favourite happy thoughts was travelling on a jumbo jet. At that time of her life, she'd never been on one and neither, of course, had I. She'd leave me in my room to grapple existentially and I'd picture the jumbo jet, at first flying in bright sunlight, then groaning off into the darkness of deep space and black eternity.

People have obviously spent a lot of time and money on the question of whether or not we're alone in the universe, but not as much on whether we're at home in it. Yet, when I watched the documentary *Invisible Universe Revealed: 25 Years of Hubble*, I couldn't help considering the second question.

The documentary tracks the history of the launch and deployment of the Hubble telescope, a scientific breakthrough on par with the one brought about by Galileo's first instrument. Beyond the havoc that earth's atmosphere plays with terrestrial telescopes, the giant and acutely accurate Hubble has answered the question of how old our universe is, confirmed the presence of black holes at the heart of virtually every galaxy, found that the universe is expanding rapidly, and offered us new, mind-blowing images of our universe.

When as a child I first considered the vastness of the universe, I was stricken, crying with horror and fear. When I looked at the images from Hubble of stars dying and being born, galaxies forming and dwarf stars shining, all of them appearing crafted by some high artisan, I almost cried at the splendour of it all. At the magnificent universe that's our home.

Coming home to God in my early twenties transformed the substance of my existential tears. It allowed me, if I tuned in, to see in a leaf, face or a star being born the same set of fingerprints. Jesus said in John's Gospel that if a person loves him they'll keep his word then the Father will love that person and they'll go and *make their home in him or her*.

God coming home to me. The high artisan of the universe saying this looks like a good place to put down roots. Forget the World/Galaxy/Universe, the view seems good from out of this young bloke who defaces Scrabble boards. And, what's more, it's a home that's undergoing renovations; Jesus says his resurrection self is off preparing for me another home, something about mansions – and plenty of them – in God's house.

Of course, all that talk of homes and houses is symbolic of some mystery that can't be fathomed, like the number of stars in the universe. Oh, but, hang on, the Hubble has revealed that: approximately ten trillion galaxies, each with approximately one hundred billion stars. Take out your calculators: we're finding out more and more about our home. We're beginning to know, even as we are known.

I had a Parkes radio telescope poster pinned to my wall throughout my teens. So, looking back on my conversion, I'm not surprised to recall that some of the action took place in the heavenlies. I saw visions of crosses in a night sky. I sang repeatedly to another stormy night sky by the beach the only Christian song I knew then, Sister Janet Mead's disco hit 'The Lord's Prayer'. Every time I came to the end of the sung prayer, *on earth as it is in heaven*, lightning flashed. The first time, a coincidence. The second, I furrowed my brow. The tenth and eleventh time – I stopped and went to bed, at home in the universe.

Space also fascinates my primary-school-aged son. He has a hardcover book called *Cosmic Menagerie*. Its pages are filled with startling images, some from Hubble. In detailed words and pictures that'll keep him busy until he's a teenager, phenomena such as stellar shockwaves, planetary nebulae and low-mass x-ray binaries are explained. He loves the book, wants it read to him nightly. But the same boy's afraid of death.

Like me, he worked out the secret early. One day at school he was told the sun would die. He realised that big events like that meant he was interminably tied into this space-time-life-death matrix: 'Dad, I'm going to die and then I'm going to be nothing and, oh, no, oh,' he stumbled, the tears starting, 'I wish I'd never been born so I didn't have to die!'

He's already been on a jumbo jet. And I've never seen such enthusiasm for life: music, sport, science, friends, animals, the environment. It's as if he's read Vincent van Gogh's adage: 'The best way to know God is to love many things.' I place my hand on his heart and tell him there's a Life in the universe, in me and in him, that never dies. That's more powerful than jumbo jets and the sun. That's more loving, even, than this man who wants to cry at your beauty and hold your heart forever safe from the fear of a dark universe where death and fear try to reign.

Well, not quite those words. But whatever they were, he seemed at home with them. And he slipped peacefully off to sleep.

28

Bill Fay: The Lowly Raised

BRITISH MUSICIAN BILL FAY 'died' as a public artist in 1971, was partially reborn in the late '90s, and finally resurrected in 2012. An up-and-coming singer-songwriter in the late '60s London music scene, Fay released an eponymous album in 1970, followed by *Time of the Last Persecution* in 1971. Though his piano-driven laments were considered worthy enough for Deram Records to release, sales were scarce and the label dropped him. Never to be heard from again. At least that's what Fay thought.

According to what he told *Spin* magazine in 2018, he was in the late '90s doing some gardening and decided to listen to some of his old albums on cassette.

'A part of me thought they were quite good. I thought, 'Maybe somebody will hear them someday'. That same evening... I got a call from a music writer telling me that my two albums were being reissued. A shock is not gonna get much bigger than that... I'd come to terms with the fact that I was deleted, but I had always kept writing songs anyway, and that was good enough...'

Those '90s reissues were repackaged again in 2005 and Fay's rebirth further flowered. Alternative music heavy hitters Nick Cave and Wilco's Jeff Tweedy tuned in to Fay's music. And with names like those getting Fay attention, it wasn't long before he garnered enough music industry cred to have a label knock on his door and ask if he'd like to record a new album.

From the outset of his career, Fay's lyrics have featured Christian imagery, even if early ones were layered with '60s psychedelic stylings. His years in the musical wilderness – when he made most of his living as a cleaner – appear to have brought hard-won wisdom to his 21st century religious lyric output, coupled with deep gratitude for his musical rebirth:

'Feel like a bird that can fly/Whose wings once were broken/I don't ask much for myself/But for the ones I love/If they should stray away from you/ Receive them back into your arms' 'Thank You Lord' – 2012

Bill Fay's 2012 album *Life is People*, his first album in forty-one years, received eight out of ten on music reviewing powerhouse *Pitchfork*, and has received similar rankings virtually everywhere else. *Pitchfork*'s reviewer, Grayson Currin, summed up the album by saying:

'*Life is People* doesn't feel at all like a late-life afterthought from a cult hero. Pointed and urgent but never pushy, Fay's songs offer pleas for redemption in a world drunk on its promise, coupled with a reassuring contentment for simply having lived this life.'

Fay was 69 when he recorded *Life is People*, a near-impossible age to suddenly be considered musically relevant, even in the alternative scene. But the album became an international hit, one he followed as successfully with *Who is the Sender?* three years later at age 72, then *Countless Branches* as a 78-year-old. Three albums of simple songs, spun on piano and guitar, backed by subtle organ and, when the big lift is needed, orchestra and choir. Virtually every song speaking from an abiding Christian faith. All from an old man whose voice is thinning, his body broken by forty years of scrubbing floors, but whose spirit, it seems, was being renewed – and healed – every day.

Many are quick to think of the lowly being raised as something for the life beyond, but Bill Fay's life in music is a reminder it can happen anytime. Along with the lift in his personal profile, the implicit and explicit Christian message flowing through Fay's melancholic music was likewise raised, brought to the attention of an alternative music audience unlikely to ever enter a church.

Incredibly, given his history of musical obscurity, Fay donated proceeds from his comeback album, *Life is People*, to medical aid organisation *Médecins Sans Frontières*/Doctors Without Borders (MSF). '*Médecins Sans Frontières* are kind of global paramedics, entering the worst possible situations going on in this world,' he told *Aquarium Drunkard* magazine when asked why he'd donated to them. 'It's difficult though, there's just so many very good organisations... there's so much good being done on this earth within situations that shouldn't exist.'

When asked about why his comeback albums were so successful, he gave most of the praise to his backing band. The albums were, he said, as much their success as his. In all his interviews, Fay is quick to praise those who've had anything to do with helping give audiences the opportunity to hear his music. He also praises his father, who took him on holidays when he was a kid and gave him the title for his first comeback album.

'We'd sit in seaside cafes and he'd watch people walking by. He was astonished at it and he would say, 'Life is people',*

Fay recalled, adding that he'd been emotionally gratified to be given an intimate view of his father's view of life.

Reading Fay's lyric sheet – and the lyric sheet of his life – it's possible to see he's also been taken into his heavenly father's view of life, and music lovers are the richer for this lowly man being raised:

'There's a rhythm and rhyme/To the years and days/There's a signature/At the bottom of the page/There's a melody/At the heart of it' – 'How Little' (2014).

29

Forever Young

'Forever young/I want to be/Forever young/Do you really want to live forever?/Forever, or never?'

THAT'S A LYRIC from German pop group Alphaville's song, released in 1984. I was sixteen and, given one of the song's lines – 'We're only watching the skies/Hoping for the best, but expecting the worst/Are you gonna drop the bomb or not?' – I should have been singing it at 'Ban the Bomb' rallies. The track should have been one of my teen anthems, but I didn't know it existed. Instead, it became a tween anthem for my daughter and eldest son; the first time I heard the song it was coming from one of their speakers in 2006, but it wasn't the original. A band well named to cover it, Youth Group, had found success with their version after it found its way onto the soundtrack to US TV series *The OC*. Then, in 2009, American rapper Jay Z released a remix of the Alphaville version to his adoring public. But that version, my now twenty-one-year-old rap aficionado son tells me, was itself a re-work of the 1992 cover of the song done by Wayne Wonder/Buju Banton/Stone Love.

Talk about self-fulfilling prophecy. 'Forever Young' seems fresh for every new music-loving audience. And that fits perfectly in the cultural milieu my youngest son occupies. For my eleven-year-old, new or old music is meaningless. It simply comes out of a phone or an iPad, right now. It has no history or future, he just hears it.

Despite the seeming agelessness of so many cultural artefacts in a digital age, no such desire for eternal youth exists in my adult children. Instead, they're aligned to that old pattern of wanting to grow up. During her former work at a café, my twenty-something daughter overheard a four-year-old girl talking to her mum. The mum explained to her daughter there were certain things she couldn't do because of her age. The girl sobbed and squealed, 'I want to be five! Everything will be better when I'm five!'

My daughter and I laughed at the little girl's pathos, but, later that day, my daughter, desperate to get finished with eternal uni and café work, said, 'I can't wait to be thirty, with a full-time job, and having brunch on the weekend.' I waited to see if she caught the irony in her statement, but no. That was probably the moment to talk to her about St Augustine's meditations on time, but the topic came up later when we chatted about what her future might hold.

'You realise that time, well, it's a construct because,' I stuttered, doing my best to explain St. A's thoughts, 'we don't know where the past or the future are, and the present never actually arrives?'

Her vague nod showed it hadn't been a subject of late-night chats with her girlfriends.

'So, yeah,' she said, 'time doesn't really exist?'

'No, probably not,' I replied, not having a clue. 'But we have to work with it.'

I'm glad she and my older son show no interest in remaining forever young, surrounded as they are by celebs keen to remain ever-youthful, to appear perfect, to never wrinkle, to never say or do anything that might show their age. Because that's not how I lived as a twenty-something – and it started in my teens.

I was ageist. Dire Straits were one of my favourite bands growing up. They played a record thirteen straight shows at the Melbourne Sports and Entertainment Centre in 1986, and I caught a gig somewhere in the middle. I was obsessed with the Straits and put on my wall a poster of Mark Knopfler playing guitar: signature red headband, sweat flying – and greying hair.

The poster was up a few months before I felt uncomfortable hero worshipping a bloke with silver locks. I pulled down the poster, got interested in younger bands or those whose lead singers had died and had no chance of getting grey hair.

But grey hair was soon to be all around me. The economy went into recession when I was joining the workforce in the early 1990s. Young people struggled to find part-time gigs, let alone full-time work. My employment history was limited to being a service station console operator and, failing to get that work, a registered nurse friend thought twenty-year-old me had a caring personality. She prised open a door that should have been closed and soon I was a nurse's assistant at an aged care facility.

Grey hair everywhere. White too. And people whose lives were ending as mine was getting started. It cured my ageism, forever. People needed spoon feeding, their soiled undergarments and bedclothes removed, those same people who told me of high-ranking former professions.

I could almost hear a voice in my ear: *This is what it comes to, Paul. Think less about what you do with your life and more about who you are in it.*

Too often, I failed to listen. Trying to be a rock star in a band in my mid-twenties, I read *Rolling Stone* magazine hyper aware of musicians' ages. How far behind was I? Our band didn't have a single or album, not even a recording contract... Then, when my creative energies turned to writing, something I was better at, the same age anxiety appeared: how old was Tim Winton when *Cloudstreet* was published? Oh my God, twenty-seven! I was thirty-three when I first noticed that fact and I hadn't even published a book...

Danae Bosler, whom I taught creative writing at university, was at time of writing this piece Mayor of the City of Yarra in her mid-twenties. A current popstar, Billie Ellish, in the forever young music industry at seventeen, had received a billion plays and had fifteen million followers on Instagram. And what about that Jesus bloke? Thirty-three and hung on a cross, and now with several billion followers – and growing – over two millennia.

But then there's Norman Maclean, who published his perfect novella *A River Runs Through It* when he was seventy-four. And Allan Gray who, at age eighty-three, was still employed as an engineer and had for ten years volunteered weekly at a St Vincent's de Paul soup van. He said, 'I know it sounds silly, but I need to go out and be educated by these people on the street.' Considered the van's wisest volunteer, he's been known to literally give the clothes off his back to people in need.

If there's one version of 'Forever Young' – hip-hop, literary, popstar or politician – that I could bear listening to forever, it's

Allan's. Youth might be wasted on the young as Oscar Wilde said, and age might be just a number as many fitness coaches shout, but I want to be forever young in the way that Allan is.

'I've got no plans of retiring,' he said. 'I jokingly say that when you retire you have an affair, you buy a boat, you paint your house and after that, what do you do? Sit in God's waiting room? You've got to plan [for that time], but I don't plan to retire. I've got too many things to do.'

30

The Book That Changed Me

I CHOSE TO DO YEAR 11 ENGLISH LITERATURE because I liked to read. It might sound a laid back way to choose a subject, but it was the only way to do it in the '80s because you didn't get any subject information, such as:

This subject will see you read a style of writing with which you haven't engaged since you were a toddler, poring over storybook rhymes. Or, this subject will introduce you to a book that'll change your life: Seven Centuries of Poetry in English, *edited by John Leonard.*

At first, my giggling peers and I pencilled rude drawings in our copies of Leonard's compendium. At my high school, students who showed the least interest in schoolwork were *ipso facto* the coolest. And I had to sketch the rudest drawings during poetry study because I was secretly the most interested student.

At home, I read *Seven Centuries'* poems in a way I later understood was close to *lectio divina*; I inhabited the works, allowed them to settle in me and lower their deep roots. I'd no religious upbringing, no belief in God, and I'd never read the Bible. But I wanted to know why on earth I was on earth. And, in *Seven Centuries*, the poets to whom I gravitated – William Blake, Emily Dickinson and T.S. Eliot – seemed to

The Book That Changed Me

be writing about something I understood as being 'beneath' physical existence:

'What are the roots that clutch, what branches grow
Out of this stony rubbish? Son of man,
You cannot say, or guess, for you know only
A heap of broken images, where the sun beats,
And the dead tree gives no shelter, the cricket no relief...'
T.S. Eliot – from 'The Waste Land'

'There came a Wind like a Bugle –
It quivered through the Grass
And a Green Chill upon the Heat
So ominous did pass
We barred the Windows and the Doors
As from an Emerald Ghost –'
Emily Dickinson – from ['There came a Wind like a Bugle']

'When the stars threw down their spears
And water'd heaven with their tears:
Did he smile his work to see?
Did he who made the Lamb make thee?'
William Blake – from 'The Tyger'

I stared out my bedroom window at Mum's rockery, its banksia, shrubs and fountain grass. What was beneath physical existence? Was it under Mum's garden? Careful to hide the fact from peers and, well, everyone, the footy playing jock that I was started writing his own versions of Blake,

Dickinson and Eliot's poems. He plumbed the universe as he knew it, scrawling plaintive doggerel, trying to write his way through to this realm beyond the rockery:

'If the doors of perception were cleansed, everything would appear to man as it is, Infinite.'
William Blake – from 'The Marriage of Heaven and Hell'

I finished Year 11 – and 12 – English Literature, but didn't put *Seven Centuries* up for sale, its rude drawings rubbed out, to a new cohort. And I kept writing poetry, until, when I turned twenty, one of them became a prayer.

Seven Centuries' poets had lit a fire and I'd been, without realising it, investigating the idea of faith in God for three years. A couple of friends, the band U2 and stray copies of *The Plain Truth* led me to think deeply about Jesus. But when preachers shouted at me on Friday nights in Geelong's CBD and scandals hit American prosperity gospellers, I couldn't see myself becoming 'Christian'.

Simultaneously, I understood my *Seven Centuries'* poets were writing about the spiritual realm. They were even, sometimes, writing to God. So, I thought I'd give that a go.

I still have the poem I addressed to God in pencil, complaining about religious violence, church hypocrites and moralists. And, to cut a blockbuster movie-style conversion story short, editing out my Blakean visions of heaven and hell, two weeks later I believed in God.

Writing and reading poetry has remained part of my spiritual journey. This week I started reading the late Denise Levertov's *The Stream and the Sapphire*, a collection of the more obviously religious poetry from her books. I listened for the spirit in her rhyme and meter, sought the Word within her words. Poets whose work engages seriously with the divine – Kevin Hart, Les Murray, Wendell Berry, Maura Eichner, Annie Dillard, R.S. Thomas, to name fewer than I want to – have helped me explore faith, doubt, heartbreak, peace and failure, made me remember that light lives in me and will break through my darkness. Which often happens through writing poetry.

I've poured my faith, doubt, rebelliousness and hope into three poetry collections. Before I published my second, I was reading from my first book, *Minorphysics*, during an event at Readings Bookshop, Hawthorn in 2006. Afterwards, a man with longish grey hair and glasses with one frame shaded black, told me how much he'd enjoyed my poetry. I said thank you and he introduced himself.

John Leonard. *Seven Centuries of Poetry in English*.

My heart didn't skip a beat, but it did some kind of gymnastic trick. Seven centuries of poetry and mine was going okay?

John gave his time to me freely as I worked on my next book, *Awake Despite the Hour*, helping me craft poems and give the manuscript shape. I've had some divine experiences in the poetry world: a masterclass with the late Les Murray where he told me my work was full of love, and feature reading my work in a famous New York poetry venue. But to get John's encouragement and guidance made me feel more than ever that my poems could help give the doors of perception a quick wipe so we can see what's beyond there, or underneath:

'I am breathing my eyes open,
air leaves me, a mist of words.
I am speaking to the breathing
air. And what the air's missing
I speak. There is no answer
to my breathing, but I hear
the flutter of a bird's wing,
the curl of a cloud through air.
This is as close as I come.'

Paul Mitchell – 'Prayer' – from *Awake Despite the Hour*.

31
In the Middle of the Madding Crowd

LIKE CELEBRITIES OF TODAY, trapped by paparazzi when leaving their homes, Jesus seems to have spent a lot of time fighting his way through crowds:

'... [T]he crowds were amazed at his teaching'; '... [L]arge crowds followed him'; 'When the crowd saw this, they were filled with awe'; 'Jesus entered the synagogue leader's house and saw the noisy crowd...'; 'A large crowd followed him, and he healed all who were ill.'

Just a few quotes from the middle of Matthew's Gospel. Later, of course, the same crowd that hails him a hero as he rides into Jerusalem on a donkey shouts for his death by crucifixion. The lesson has always been a simple one: don't trust the crowd. As quick as it'll build you up, it'll cut you down.

Today's crowds at sporting events, protest rallies and concerts are much bigger than those Jesus confronted, and he also didn't have the 24-7 social media crowd. The social media crowd, like a live one, has millions of individual voices, but, unlike a live crowd, you can listen to each one in it as it builds you up or tears you down at a keystroke.

There's a story, maybe a global village myth, of a company CEO who tweeted a remark before boarding an international flight. After twenty hours without internet access, she landed in her destination to find an angry crowd venting at her about her remark, and to receive the news she'd been sacked.

When I was in Grade Four at a state primary school, the teacher gave us a lesson in thinking for ourselves. Relating what might also have been a myth, she told us there had once been an experiment in which ten people were gathered in a room around a large table. On that table were several bright blue carrots. Nine people had been told to pretend that bright blue was a carrot's natural colour. The other person in the room was of the standard belief that carrots were normally orange. The nine convinced him otherwise.

The crowd for years sang the praises of Aung Sun Suu Kyi then, discovering she couldn't stand up to the Myanmar military, tore her down. The crowd sang New Zealand Prime Minister Jacinda Arden's praises for handling her nation's mosque massacre with grace and dignity. At time of writing, New Zealanders weren't so sure of Arden's saintliness.

'If all your friends were running off a cliff, would you jump off too?' mum quizzed me whenever I asked if I could have a treat my primary school friends were having. 'No, I wouldn't,' I said, looking painfully at my friend's ice-cream. Now, as an adult, I wait and wait before saying anything on social media because, hey, look at this: someone just posted a photo of what appears to be several local parking inspectors peering at a car's tyres to see if the owner should be issued with an infringement. The post's comments feed goes wild, ripping into parking inspectors from Footscray to Finland. The next day it emerges the parking inspectors were police officers collecting evidence of a stolen vehicle. The crowd didn't apologise, it just rolled to the next outrage.

Senator Fraser Anning made comments in the wake of the aforementioned New Zealand massacres with which I had no sympathy. Along with many Australians, I'm not pleased our political system allows him – or anyone – into the senate with only a handful of votes. But the crowd had an idea about how to change the system. It genuinely believed that if it got enough signatures it could throw Anning out of office. And why wouldn't it think that were possible? Our politicians are only too willing to deal with hard-basket questions like marriage equality by taking them to a referendum, telling the crowd to vote because the people it chose to represent them refused to govern.

Hands up who wants marriage equality? Hands up who wants Fraser Anning out? Hands up if you think carrots are bright blue? The crowd, rolling and restless. It wants quick answers, absolute justice, and offers no forgiveness. Give us Barabbas! Crucify Jesus!

Crucify Tayla Harris, Carlton AFLW footballer. Famously photographed kicking a ball in the game she loves, she faced a huge crowd of keyboard wimps, mocking her gender, mocking her sport, and mocking her. She stood strong, it took guts, the crowd disappeared – but then reappeared, racially taunting an AFL male player. Would there be anything wrong with not offering a comment feed under every article or image ever published? True, it would also mean we'd lose positive comments, but it would suck away some of the obviously polluted air digital trolls need to stay alive.

In an article in *The Age* challenging the hold tribalism has on political debate in the US, Matthew Knott reported that twenty per cent of Democrats and sixteen per cent of Republicans believed the US would be better off if large numbers of those who vote for the opposition party died. This was in an article pointing out that Australian commentators who'd expressed moderate or nuanced points of view in the wake of the New Zealand mosque massacre had been savagely pilloried by both left and right.

The crowd's everywhere and has never been larger or had bigger megaphones. The crowd's extreme, it doesn't work with nuance or credit where credit's due. It pushes civil debate on any issue to the margins, while opposing crowd members throw grenades across the trenches.

The choice? Join one side of the crowd and throw your bombs, or stay in the trench, open to truth whatever its source might be, open to hearing another's point of view, copping flak from either direction, flak that may eventually build up to the point that it's covering your mouth, but you keep answering questions with questions, seeking truth, being truth, because truth makes no other claim than it'll set you free from whatever the crowd's screaming now and whatever new thing it'll scream tomorrow.

Easier said than done, as Adam Goodes realised. Easier said than done, as Jesus found out. Easier said than done, as Martin Luther King learned. Easier said than done, as Rosa Parks came to understand. Easier said than done, as Tayla Harris discovered. The list of names goes on, but, importantly, we know them. We respect them. We even honour them. The names of the crowd? Anonymous, trolling, falling over themselves to be on the side they think's winning, forgotten by history, the many finally silenced voices of the bleating mob.

32

The Abbot of the Household

ONCE UPON A SUNNY YEAR, I enjoyed three days at a rural monastery. I gazed at the idyllic view of lake, pasture and cows, and chatted with a monk about life, the universe, families and prayer. He suggested I should see myself as the Abbot of my little household, which then included my wife, three-year-old son, and two visiting early teens from my first marriage. In the monastery's pristine conditions, the monk's idea seemed as easy as the honey-eaters' whip and whorl around the garden's banksia bushes. But at home, the Abbot-hood he'd bestowed upon me confronted the rise and fall of my spiritual see-saw.

With a fourteen-year-old daughter interested in what God might mean for her life – and asking questions about faith – I saw it was risky to base the discussion on my personal experience, those many dark nights and occasional bright dawns of the soul. I tried Bible reading with her from a number of versions, chats about Christian values and morals, and expositions of the lives of heroes of the faith, including Martin Luther King, St. Francis and Mother Teresa. She's now in her twenties and I can't be sure if any of those stalks of potential insight bore fruit, but I know one idea I put into action during that period did: the 'God's Heart Prayer', as my daughter so named it.

If you've read this book in order, you'll know about the God's Heart Prayer. If you haven't', here's your recap.

The prayer was cobbled together from something I read at the back of a book of mystical theology and my own intuitions of what might make a successful prayer for my daughter. A sporty and intellectual type, I thought it best the prayer engaged her brain and physicality; it should be something her thoughts could hold and that inhabited her body.

It went like this: nearly ready for sleep, she lay on her bed in her pyjamas and I began by touching her forehead lightly and saying, 'May you think God's thoughts'. Then I touched her eyelids and said, 'See with God's eyes' before touching her lips and saying, 'And speak the word of truth to yourself and others.' Then it was time for the itchy nose touch – 'Smell God's wonderful earth' – and a quick wiggle of an ear, 'Listen to what God wants and do it.' A tap on her shoulder came next, along with, 'Only carry what you need to carry', then a light touch on her tummy: 'Only stomach what you need to stomach'. Then followed a quick grip – 'May your hands be quick to heal' – and a squeeze of her toes – 'May your feet be fast to run and do what God wants...' to which I'd taught her to say: 'Love kindness, do justice and walk humbly with God'. Finally, my palm in the middle of her chest: 'May you love with God's heart'.

When she left my house at the end of Year 10 to live permanently with her mum, my soul went moonless, but I consoled myself with the fact that, during a family counselling session, my daughter had revealed she used the 'God's Heart Prayer' wherever she went. Recently, I asked her if she still recited it and the answer was yes. Though it never caught on with my eldest son, my Abbot-self today feels the 'God's Heart Prayer' is one achievement he can pin on his cloister door.

On that same trip to the monastery, I bought a small gift for each of my children to hopefully inspire them in their faith. I got my then three-year-old son a tiny colourful cross-shaped wooden pendant, depicting a stylised South American Christ. My son found it intriguing and, because he didn't like the thing flipping around when he wore it, he hung it on his bedpost. It stayed there gathering dust and sleep until one night when he was older he asked me what it was. This led to my Abbot-self delivering a poorly developed theological talk for primary school kids – until I remembered the 'God's Heart Prayer'.

My son took to it like a monk to chanting and soon it was a nightly routine – but with a difference to my daughter's. Where she allowed the prayer's statements their hang time, my youngest wanted to know what I meant by each of them. '*How* do you think God's thoughts?' 'What does only *stomach* what you need to stomach mean?' I don't know whether it was because I'd many years' experience with the prayer, but I found explaining each section easier than explaining Bible stories, offering moral narratives, or finding heroes of the faith who might matter to him.

We finally got around to baptising the young man Catholic. House moves, career moves and daughter and older son moves had all got in the way. At a celebratory lunch – and afterwards strolling the city footpath – the boy held his baptismal candle out in front of him like a baton, ready to share with all those in the world running the race of faith. It wasn't lit at the time, but he said of his candle, 'I want this to stay lit up always.'

Out of the mouths of babes – and also from their fingertips. That night, his candle lit beside his bed, we went through the

'God's Heart Prayer', thinking God's thoughts, figuring out what we needed to carry and stomach, and how healing might happen. I'd always added at the end of my daughter's prayer a last touch to her forehead and the words, 'May God's love be with you – and my love too.' I continued that routine with my youngest son. That night, perhaps honouring his time at the Baptismal font with the priest, he licked his index finger and made the sign of the cross on my forehead, then did the same on his own.

My Abbot-self smiled, blew out my son's candle, but felt it might indeed remain forever lit.

33
How to Protect the Gift

MY DAUGHTER TURNED TWENTY-ONE. At her age, I spent some weekends with friends on Victoria's surf coast, staying at a house with panoramic views of Bass Strait, with plenty of alcohol to keep our conversations buoyant. I'd just come to faith in God, always had a lot to say, probably too much; life's meaning was always high on our agenda and I was instrumental in putting it there. The morning after one of our long nights getting high and low on booze and meaning, I saw we'd been busy the previous night scrawling diagrams and writing on pieces of paper. A sentence drew my eye, one that over the subsequent thirty years has grown in importance:

The earth is a gift.

I laughed when I read it. It was so far removed from our concerns: capitalism v socialism; religion v atheism; the birth of the European Union; Perestroika in the USSR; and the question of what the hell we were all going to do with our lives. But, according to my daughter, only the mystery writer of the gift statement had the right agenda.

'You guys *knew* what was happening with climate change. What did you do about it?' she said over dinner in Lygon Street, close to the university at which she was then studying a subject that asked her to think about why Australia's energy policy was polarised when the climate science was in – and had been for ages.

I told her when I'd turned twenty-one, I'd just come off the back of protesting the threat of global nuclear war. Climate change hadn't then penetrated the mushroom cloud in which Generation X was enveloped. I asked my daughter how she felt about the future – and a real bomb hit.

'I think we're stuffed, actually,' she said.

There was no imminent threat of death at the table, but her life flashed before my eyes: fluffy hair in her cot, in uniform for her first day at school, a key member of a national rowing crew, and her twenty-first birthday party just months before.

I managed to polish the rest of my spaghetti marinara, hopefully sustainably caught, but I didn't feel much like eating. I hadn't raised her on this gift of an earth to feel she might be one of the last of her species to walk upon it.

◊ ◊ ◊

In his non-fiction book *The Great Derangement: Climate Change and the Unthinkable*, novelist Amitav Ghosh tells why he thinks we so easily put climate change aside. And he brings his literary eye to two significant climate documents, the Paris Agreement and Pope Francis's *Laudato Si'* encyclical.

Ghosh writes that people might expect the Paris Agreement to be hard-headed, while the *Laudato Si'* would be full of wishful thinking. But he points out that the Paris Agreement more often invoked the impossible: 'For example, the aspirational goal of limiting the rise in global mean temperatures to 1.5 degrees Centigrade – a target that is widely believed to be already beyond reach.'

Ghosh says the Paris Agreement effectively asks us to trust that technological advances, many of which are in their infancy, will save us from climate change's full impact. 'The most promising of them', he writes, 'biomass energy carbon capture and storage', would require the planting of bioenergy crops over an area larger than India to succeed at scale. To invest so much trust in what is yet only a remote possibility is little less than an act of faith...'

By contrast, Ghosh says the *Laudato Si'* makes no case for miraculous interventions. 'It strives instead to make sense of humanity's present predicament by mining the wisdom of a tradition that far predates the carbon economy.' He highlights the fact that the Pope takes issue with past erroneous positions on the environment the Church has taken, at the same time as he's scathing about the notion that unlimited growth can function alongside ecological concern, which the Paris Agreement suggests is possible.

Ghosh's work drove me to the *Laudato Si'* and I read it in full, finding that eighteen times it talked of the earth and life as gifts. It was impossible to come away unmoved by its depth of inquiry and its clear calls for global political, spiritual and social change. The *Laudato Si'* tells us that to be people of any faith – to even be human – in this current age cannot be separated from individual and social action to mitigate the effects of climate change.

'Once we start to think about the kind of world we are leaving to future generations, we look at things differently; we realise that the world is a gift which we have freely received and must share with others,' Pope Francis writes. 'Since the world has been given to us, we can no longer view reality in a purely utilitarian way, in which efficiency and productivity are entirely geared to our individual benefit.'

Pope Francis criticises political policies that damage the environment, clear in his assessment that there's no argument about the climate science, and uncompromising in his call for all humanity, but especially people of faith, to see there's no greater issue to deal with in our lifetimes. He also points out that we can't make inroads on any other global social concern – from poverty to war – without dealing effectively with climate change.

Amitav Ghosh makes the point in *The Great Derangement* that most of history's other major social justice victories, from the abolishment of slavery to the campaign for Civil Rights in America and its global flow-on, were precipitated upon slow-burn, grass roots movements. He says when it comes to climate change action, there's no time for that; the action needed will have to come from existing groups.

The leader of one of the world's largest social groups has given an unequivocal message: change our ways or risk the gift of life on earth.

'Living our vocation to be protectors of God's handiwork is essential to a life of virtue,' Pope Francis writes, 'it is not an optional or a secondary aspect of our Christian experience.'

According to Pope Francis, my daughter and I have to stop the blame game and remember that the very spirit of God empowers our efforts. We *can* hope and believe that together we can protect the gift. Climate action is an intergenerational concern that, as the school climate strikes have shown, must see children, parents and grandparents together on the front lines of action.

'Intergenerational solidarity is not optional, but rather a basic question of justice,' Pope Francis writes. 'We may well be leaving to coming generations debris, desolation and filth. The pace of consumption, waste and environmental change has so stretched the planet's capacity that our contemporary lifestyle, unsustainable as it is, can only precipitate catastrophes, such as those which even now periodically occur in different areas of the world. The effects of the present imbalance can only be reduced by our decisive action, here and now.'

34

No Fear for Little Monsters

I HADN'T PLANNED on a monster hunt with my ten-year-old son. It was spring school holidays and we were carefree, ambling a sunlit and empty road to Sandy Point's wide open beach. But we'd definitely heard a monster-like snort from somewhere along a street to our right.

'What was *that*?' my son shouted, almost dropping his body board.

In his wetsuit, he tugged me away from the monster's roar, toward the other side of the road and the thorny green scrub. I laughed. Whoops, wrong move. Stern eyes below blond hair told me this was no time for jokes. I was supposed to be protecting him.

But he was raised in the city and I was raised in country Victoria. He didn't realise there was nothing to be scared of. Well, not really.

'What do you think it is?' I asked him.

'A giant pig?'

It sounded like a wild boar, ready to thrust its tusks into him...

'It's not a pig...'

I guided his reluctant steps along the bitumen to a eucalyptus sapling out front of a beach shack. The tree's branches were so young the monster was bending the one on which it sat. My son dropped his body board.

'A *ko-a-la*!' he said with a smile as wide as his vowels.

'Have you ever seen one?' I asked him, unsure of the zoos we'd visited.

'Not like this... in the street!'

The fluffy monster chomped on fresh, green leaves and stared at my son. They eyed each other for ten minutes. The boy had been keen to get to the surf, but I had to almost drag him to the waves.

Back at home in Melbourne's inner west, nature isn't a big part of his life. There's a ringtail possum which, now he's realised it won't hurt him, he likes to watch when he can. It lives in the Banksia Rose bush beside his bedroom window. Sometimes in the city haze that offers something like the cover of darkness, the possum tightropes our paling fence on a mission to steal peaches from our tree.

My son also does the annual Birds Australia Backyard Bird Count, sitting for twenty minutes on a deckchair and taking notes on an app about what he sees. Amongst intruder species of pigeons, sparrows and Indian Mynahs, he squawks when he spots native ravens, parrots and, once, a pelican.

But his experience of nature is mostly two-dimensional: David Attenborough on TV and newsletters from Wildlife Victoria. Outside this virtual contact, he'd started to develop a fear of nature I worried was a result of having so little contact with it.

He'd become terrified of snakes, which isn't unusual in his age group. I mean, there aren't many around who love them. But even really young kids don't worry about them like my son had started to, unless those kids happened to be swishing through long grass on a hot day.

When we went back to Sandy Point for summer holidays, it was wise to have healthy respect for snakes. Signs were everywhere warning visitors about tiger snakes, that species responsible for many of the nation's bites, about sixty per cent of which are fatal. And, unfortunately, my son and his cousins had spotted one in September, off in beachside scrub. So when on our summer arrival I suggested we go check the surf, see if it was worth hauling our boards up the hilly bush track, he didn't want any part of it.

'Too many snakes.'

'You've only seen *one* in the wild.'

'I'm not going.'

Relatives were, as always, staying close by, so I tried a new move in this game of Snakes and Beaches.

'What if your cousins come with us?'

'I'm not going.'

I ran him through Snakes in the Bush 101: we carry a stick with us, we stay on the track, we speak loudly and thump our footsteps. If a snake's on the track, we wait for it to leave. If it won't leave, we throw something in its direction and it'll slither off.

'I've only seen one snake in the wild,' I told him. 'I was hiking and a brown snake took off in front of me.'

I didn't tell him Eastern browns are deadlier than tiger snakes. But I decided full disclosure was vital and so I told him about the snake I hadn't seen, but wish I had.

'A water snake bit me in New Caledonia. But that was only because there were no signs up. Do you think I'd have gone swimming if there were signs?'

'Did it hurt?'

'Like hell.'

'What other animals have bitten you?'

'An emu.'

'An emu!?' he gasped, and I sensed him forming a picture of the unwieldy bird aiming its long-necked, toothless peck.

'Yep, in a nature park. Bit me on the arm.'

He looked for the wound.

'It was a long time ago.'

Something about me surviving the emu bite encouraged him and we made for the beach track. We thumped past the snake warning signs, holding our sticks and chattering loudly. The waves looked okay, but the wind was about to change and turn the surf to custard.

Heading back to our holiday hut, I saw what I thought was a cat on the paling fence among the eucalyptuses between our place and the one next door. The feline looked well-fed.

'Look at that huge cat,' I pointed. It was so big we wanted to see it up close. Yes, definitely a monster. Just like the one he'd seen last school holidays. 'It's a ko-a-la!'

He was straight inside the house and I was worried he was scared again, but I happily realised he was dashing for the backyard and a better view.

'He's so cute,' my son purred, and my wife appeared from the bedroom, still in pyjamas. We stood in the backyard and watched this muscular bundle of fur grip bark with strong paws and clamber for the top of the tree, where it would likely sleep all day.

'*He's* not functionally extinct,' I said, thinking of bushfire photos then doing the rounds on social media. So many koalas with blistered paws and singed ears, sitting helpless on scorched earth. Thousands had died in the bushfires that were then still ripping through the south, but I struggled to comprehend the idea that they were critically endangered.

'Do you want to sponsor a koala?' my wife asked my son, obviously thinking of the charities getting to work trying to save them. My son looked engaged enough in his furry friend's plight to climb the tree and hang out with him all day.

'Yes, definitely,' he said.

The koala eventually crawled high into the gum tree and out of sight. Later, the wind changed and my son grabbed his body board and headed to the beach with his cousins, without a word about snakes.

35

Stuck in a Moment

IN AN INTERVIEW ONCE, U2's Bono implored western governments to take more seriously the plight of millions of Africans that AIDS was affecting. He told governments to get off their collective backsides, while at the same time describing depression as a Western illness brought about by a lack of meaning and purpose.

His central message was that Westerners get depressed because they have too much stuff and not enough meaning. If we had to struggle just to survive, like so many in the developing world, we wouldn't have time to be depressed. And if we took time to think about the rest of humanity's needs, we'd discover that the warm glow of giving can thaw depression's submerged iceberg.

I wish this were true, but it hasn't been my experience.

I've had depression, on and off and in different degrees, since I was eight. Apart from my parents, it's been my longest and closest companion, one I didn't recognise as living with me until I was twenty-eight, and a condition I've been managing with medication and counselling ever since. And, like an old school companion, no sooner do you think you've lost contact forever than he rings up and says, 'Mind if I come and stay for a few weeks? Actually, make that a few months, if that's okay?'

When my old companion comes to stay, he really messes up my house. You can't leave him alone for a minute or he'll have everything on the floor, strewn around or smashed, and you'll be picking up the pieces, while he's there and after he's gone.

I know when he's arrived to visit because I'm irritable and snappy. I don't answer the phone and I find it hard to be in people's company. I can't sleep properly and I'm plagued by feelings of total failure – in everything from cleaning the house to parenting; nothing's fun to do or even think about doing.

When Bono wrote 'Stuck in a Moment', his song about former INXS frontman Michael Hutchence's suicide, he was, despite his documented suspicion about depression's causes, well aware his mate had found himself in a psychological situation from which he could see no exit. Interviewed about the song, Bono said the lyric was a fictional argument between friends: himself, and Hutchence on the verge of suicide. It makes you hear the song's chorus in a different way:

Bono: 'You've got to get yourself together, you're stuck in a moment and you can't get out of it'

Hutchence: 'Don't say that later will be better...'

'In the song,' Bono said in an interview, 'I'm right there – I wanted to have that argument in that half an hour... Can you really be that busy that you don't notice your mate on the slide? I just remember feeling this overwhelming sense of guilt [when he heard of Hutchence's death].'

I'm told in counselling I need to have people in my life who understand me and my condition enough that they can be there for me in that half hour. When it arrived for me once –

and I experienced desolation so intense it felt like my mind and soul had already turned into the concrete that would surely later house my body – I had someone there for me, someone who was able to keep vigil with me.

Did Michael Hutchence have someone he could ask to keep watch on him? Did this man, who'd in a chat with Bono agreed with him that suicide was 'pathetic', ever confess to a friend his desire to end his life? He had lots of 'stuff': money, fame, relationships, and houses around the world. Maybe he didn't have enough meaning...

But maybe he did.

I found myself in Hutchence's half an hour during a period of separation from my later to become ex-wife. While major life events like separation, divorce or the death of a relative or friend can obviously precipitate deep sadness and the potential for suicide, I did have other meaning in my life.

I had two kids who'd let me know they needed me and wanted me around. I had work as a writer that was at least sometimes meaningful. I had family ties and, most importantly according to the literature that highlights the role of meaning as a temper against suicide, I belonged to something larger than myself: a church community. Even if I hadn't believed in God, so the argument goes, belonging to a group in this way would create a meaning barrier that suicide would find it difficult to leap. But, as an added stave against potential suicide caused by cosmic meaninglessness, I *did* believe in God. I believe in a faithful, cosmic love existing for all of us – even resurrection. Yet I still felt like the living dead on my friend's couch that night.

I can't speak about other religions, political beliefs or systems, but I know it's not a new thing that meaning, even the religious kind, is unable to provide sure protection from depression and suicide. But it seems liberal, social justice-orientated Christians (Bono's ilk who say just get on with giving and depression will fade) and conservative Christians (just pray more, read your Bible more or cast out demons and you'll get rid of depression) may have forgotten about the lives of Christians like English poet William Cowper:

'Man disavows, and Deity disowns me:/Hell might afford my miseries a shelter;/Therefore hell keeps her ever hungry mouths all bolted against me.' (from 'Lines Written During a Period of Insanity' – William Cowper)

Any person of faith who's suffered from depression knows what Cowper's describing. And they also know that it's not enough to just categorise their depression as the 'dark night of the soul' that St John of the Cross famously described. Clinical depression seems never to leave you alone, that old school friend knocking on your door, often when you least expect it. One of my bouts of depression began on the night of my eldest son's birth.

There are numerous ways we're trying to treat depression and the threat of suicide: medication, counselling, meditation, deeper life meaning systems and ECG. As yet, however, no sure-fire way has emerged to tame the black dog. But I'm at least evidence that having someone there for you when you're on the brink is an important way of putting the black dog in its kennel. Blaming sufferers' lack of meaning, their Western 'selfishness', is another way, but it will risk making people keep their illness to themselves. And they'll keep facing their darkest half hour alone, convinced they're stuck in a moment and they can't get out of it.

36

The Preppie

1. A metamorphosis. Or good cluck to him.

HE WAS SOON TO START SCHOOL, become a preppie, but he wanted to be a hen. He wanted to be a hen and lay eggs and have chicks. He was disappointed that he wasn't a hen and that he couldn't, therefore, lay the eggs, have the chicks and care for them and cuddle them.

We had a pet. Even though we weren't supposed to have one because we rented our house. Our cat, called Moorie, named after Japanese writer Haruki Murakami, came with the house. He hung around, wouldn't leave, behaved badly. We registered him, gave him a collar, and he started behaving beautifully. We rented our house for seven years and Moorie died of kidney failure just before the preppie was set to start school.

I wondered if the preppie would still want to be a hen if we got another pet. Maybe not, but I hoped he kept coming up with creative ideas. He was already playing piano by ear and he invented games: one day he was a possum in the lounge room, crawling in and out of large, empty cardboard boxes and under the couch cushions for hours.

I was scared he'd go to school and lose his creativity. My other two did, sort of. Maybe it was just the iPad, XBox and friends who stole that quiet time in which they used to do the things that the wannabe hen did. Maybe it had nothing to do with school.

A month before the preppie was set to start his schooling life, I met a woman who'd gone to primary school in Sydney. She and her classmates had learnt whatever took their interest. She had a job now, a reasonably creative one. I was pretty sure the school my preppie was going to didn't let them learn whatever they wanted, but that's how he was learning at home. If it took his interest he'd learn it until he'd asked us more questions than a year's-worth of *Family Feud* episodes. It could start a family feud sometimes.

Maybe it was time to hand him over to the teachers and let them handle the questions. Australian poet Kristin Henry wrote about a nephew of hers on the brink of starting school: 'We gave him to you perfect' she wrote. I'm sure my preppie wasn't perfect because I don't believe in it. We have an imperfect education system for imperfect kids. But it didn't stop this father hen wanting his preppie to stay, deep down, the beautiful creative chick he was.

2. Free range

The preppie-to-be had just finished a weekend free-ranging at a relative's property adjacent bushland. He'd played basketball, skateboarded and run madly around the acres. I was out fishing in a canoe, enjoying the far reaches of the lake, when the preppie asked his Mum, 'Why haven't we got a big backyard like this?' She dodged the answer she could give: son, it's your parents' financial situation, brought about via their previous relationship breakdowns. She just told him it's because we live in the city. But that didn't stop his desire for a big backyard – or his enjoyment of the heartbreaking freedom he was experiencing. Heartbreaking? Yes, for me. The preppie was set to start school the next Friday and I felt what he didn't: that his childhood freedom was about to end.

After the preppie's siblings' positive experience of primary – and secondary – school, I thought I'd put away this fear. But no. The ghost of my own experience of primary school – in four different towns, struggling to fit in – was in uniform, haunting me. But the preppie was like John Howard in a banana lounge: relaxed and comfortable.

They say kids are sponges. If that's true, the preppie was a maxi-size one you use to clean super trucks. After watching the tennis on TV, he not only went out back to play, he impersonated the ball boys between points with quick step running and kneeling on the sidelines. I didn't want him sponging up my fears. I wanted him sponging up confidence, a sense of possibility and the joys of childhood.

But I still worried he could lose his freedom. Yet I've come slowly to realise freedom is something you carry around inside you. An egg ready to hatch. A kid ready for school.

3. *Silly chook*

The teacher said the preppie was being silly. Not naughty, she emphasised, just silly. Talking when she was talking. Not listening when she was giving instructions. Making crazy sounds and getting others involved.

The silliness lasted several days. I was doing all the pick-ups and I dreaded the teacher's next instalment: 'He was better this morning, but he went silly this afternoon.' The preppie's teacher had a system of green and red *dojos* for behaviour. I'd always thought a dojo was a martial arts centre, but, she was teaching prep and probably needed as many controls as possible. Anyway, green meant good, red bad. The preppie kept getting a mixture. 'He laughs when he gets a red one... He said sorry about what he did wrong, but he didn't mean it.' If I knew the preppie, he'd decided to get a mixture because he was fascinated with the system. Finally, he got all reds and was put in time out in another classroom.

The preppie's mum and I discussed the issue: either he was boundary testing or there was another factor at play. Perhaps his teacher was too strict. She was also the prep coordinator and needed to run a tight ship. Maybe his learning style was different. His mum hadn't listened at school unless she was interested, and would catch up learn the uninteresting stuff later. Maybe he had learning difficulties or problems paying attention. I'd seen thirty kids at Milo Cricket give their attention to the coach while the preppie had sat facing the other direction for the entire speech.

We decided to keep a close eye on things and to talk to his teacher at his early term assessment.

Before school the next day, I had another eye-to-eye chat with the preppie. 'People know you're listening if you look in their face when they're talking. Don't talk when the teacher is talking, put your hand up...' The preppie nodded.

After school, the preppie's teacher rounded on me after my son had given me his traditional end of day hug around the thighs. 'We had a much better day today', the teacher said. She explained the result to me in dojos, but it was all Kung Fu to me. 'And we found out something about you, didn't we?' The preppie looked aghast. 'What?' he implored, looking up at his two authority figures. 'We found out that you are a very clever boy!'

It turned out the preppie's silliness was down to boredom. Unlike many in his class, he could read, count to high numbers and spell biggish words. And he had a high interest in what words like 'accessory' meant. There was no more silliness. Just talk from the preppie's teacher about cleverness.

The preppie's paternal grandmother had once said we should get him checked out, and I'd groaned. The preppie's grandmother can sometimes be what I'd call an amateur GP, and she's run a successful practice since before Google. I'd asked her what we should get checked out, thinking it might be anaemia or peanut phobia. 'In case he's a genius!' she laughed.

And we'd laughed back. Most preppies are geniuses in most parents' and grandparents' eyes. But it was good to know ours wasn't silly.

4. Gathering you under my wing

Towards the end of the year, a new song began playing each morning on the primary school's PA system. All year, songs had been belted out as a way to let straggler parents and kids know the bell to start the day would soon beep.

To my ear, the new song's chorus was *All we need is hope...* I couldn't make out the rest. For two reasons: I was hurrying along with the preppie to make sure he wasn't late, and the lyric put a lump in my throat that I swallowed quickly.

I was still my son's main school-day carer. And it was a year during which the second half was dominated by acts of terrorism around the world.

For the first time, I properly registered the fact that there were people on the planet who, given the opportunity, would kill the preppie and me because we didn't want the kind of world they wanted. To my mind, that was a war footing.

It wasn't a pleasant reality with which to engage. I started to feel a presence looming over us as I helped the preppie with his homework or I read him a story at night. An unnamed threat that would willingly expunge the preppie from the earth as if he were an army commander.

The whole time I was telling myself I shouldn't think like this. That I was letting the terrorists win. Well, I'm sorry, but they did have a little victory over me, for a few months.

But it didn't last.

At the height of allowing this looming presence to darken my time with the preppie, the aforementioned hurry-up song came on the PA on our way into school. And all I saw around me was hope.

The schoolyard was filled with chattering preppies, running to their classrooms, eyes shining and faces open. They were yet to absorb the scale of tragedy life on earth could hold. And they had, I trusted, a limited awareness that some people in the world saw even their little existences as a threat.

As I watched those preppies swarm the schoolyard, full of the hope that the song embodied, I was overwhelmed. Their innocence was a force.

Instead of swallowing the lump in my throat, I let it do what it wanted. And, surprisingly, it didn't result in a rush of tears. I felt myself instead made fragile, as fragile and innocent for a moment as all those little kids around me, their lives stretching out ahead of them. Trusting their teachers, their parents and their communities to guide them and protect them. To show them, effectively, the way to live.

The Preppie

The way to live is not to allow a looming and unpredictable threat of death to dominate my thinking. Because death, via terrorists, disease, injury or old age, is always looming.

Even if it is painful and feels sometimes impossible, the way to live is with hope. The very hope with which those little ears were being instilled as they raced off to their days of learning how to spell, count, jump ropes and, as the signs on their classroom doors said, practice random acts of kindness.

I wanted to embrace them all. Instead, I simply hugged the preppie at my side, trusting it added to the sum total of hope he could have for the future.

Acknowledgments

Many essays in this collection were published in journals, magazines and news media, some under different names and in slightly different versions. My thanks to all the editors:

- Shopping for Values: A Journey with my Daughter, *Kill Your Darlings*, Issue 1, 2010.
- Dad Radio, *Sunday Life, The Age*, 2017.
- Anzacism: Lessons in a Civil Religion, *ABC Religion and Ethics*, 2015.
- Heart Prayer, *The Sunday Age*, Faith, 2011.
- Reality Check, *The Big Issue*, 2013.
- Father's Day Music Club, *The Guardian Australia*, 2020.
- Taking the Poison Out of Masculinity, *The Melbourne Catholic*, 2019.
- Ripe for the Picking, *The Age*, Epicure, 2011.
- Cuisines of the World and Crazy Thursday, *The Age* Epicure, 2010.
- Two Bobs' Worth, *The Big Issue*, 2015.
- Play it Again, This Time with Feeling, *The Age*, Life and Style, 2013.
- Dad's Kitchen Rules, *The Guardian Australia*, 2020.
- Memories, Like Some Corners of Our Lives, *The Melbourne Catholic*, 2018.
- UFC (Ultimate Fathering Confusion), *The Big Issue*, 2017.
- Punt Flick, *The Big Issue*, 2017.
- We Have the Touch, *The Melbourne Catholic*, 2017.
- When the Neighbourhood's Heart Broke, *The Age*, 2008.

- The Cracks in Our Stars, *The Melbourne Catholic*, 2018.
- The Tale Food Tells, *The Age*, Epicure, 2011.
- A Quartet of Hope, *The Melbourne Catholic*, 2019.
- A Christmas Carol Confession, *The Sunday Age*, Faith, 2010.
- It's an Emergency. Take a Seat., *Going Down Swinging* online, 2015.
- Competing to be Normal, *The Melbourne Catholic*, 2017.
- The Home Monastery, *The Melbourne Anglican*, 2020.
- Silence is Not Always Golden, *The Melbourne Catholic*, 2018.
- Everything Under the Sun, *The Melbourne Catholic*, 2018.
- Bill Fay: The Lowly Raised, *The Melbourne Catholic*, 2019.
- Forever Young, *The Melbourne Catholic* 2019.
- The Book That Changed Me, *The Melbourne Anglican*, 2020.
- In the Middle of the Madding Crowd, *The Melbourne Catholic*, 2019.
- The Abbot of the Household, *The Melbourne Catholic*, 2019.
- How to Protect the Gift, *The Melbourne Catholic*, 2018.
- Stuck in a Moment, *The Melbourne Anglican*, 2014.
- The Preppie (final section), *Eureka Street*, 2016.

The quote at the beginning of the book is from Elizabeth Alexander's poem 'Ars Poetica #56: Bullfrogs Was Falling Out of the Sky' from her book *Crave Radiance: New and Selected Poems 1990 – 2010* (Graywolf Press, 2010).